Praise for GOD IS MY COACH:

"Larry Julian has done it again with GOD IS MY COACH. His new book will help you navigate the 'gray zone'—those situations when it's hard to discern the right thing to do. Larry's biblically based leadership principles will have an enormous impact on your life."

—Pat Williams, senior vice president, Orlando Magic,
and author of *The Pursuit*

"Today's business cultures promote 'all or nothing' thinking where it's simply never enough—we're always achieving but never satisfied. Larry Julian shows us that it's the process, not the outcome, which determines our true meaning and success. GOD IS MY COACH teaches us that leading a life of purpose and running a profitable business can be one and the same."

—Horst Schulze, president & CEO, West Paces Hotel Group,
and former CEO, Ritz Carlton Hotels

"How do you combine faith, calling, and career into a comprehensive but practical process? Larry Julian shows you how in GOD IS MY COACH. There are too many books on faith and work that fail to deliver practical application. This book delivers! A must for serious marketplace leaders who want to fulfill their destinies."

—Os Hillman, author of *TGIF: Today God Is First* and *The 9 to 5 Window*

"Impatience and pressure often lead to poor decisions and burnout. Larry Julian teaches us how to use time and pressure to our advantage as part of God's plan. GOD IS MY COACH provides us with the peace of mind necessary to make tough decisions under pressure."

—Archie Dunham, chairman & CEO (Ret.), Conoco Inc.

"GOD IS MY COACH is a handbook on how to tackle uncertainty in life. In engaging true-life examples, Larry Julian shares how a life lived with purpose leaves a lasting legacy."

—John D. Beckett, chairman, The Beckett Companies

"As leaders, we're called to serve rather than be served. GOD IS MY COACH shows us how to use our gray circumstances as a training ground for effective leadership. By following God in our uncertainty, we learn how to lead others though their uncertainty."

—Wayne Huizenga, Jr., president, Miami Dolphins

continued . . .

"GOD IS MY COACH is an outstanding guide for leaders who want to know and do the right thing under pressure. Using solid biblical principles instead of the 'systems of this world' will help you and your business stand the test of time. This book will help you establish a firm foundation."

—Anne Beiler, founder, Auntie Anne's Pretzels, and author of *Twist of Faith*

"If you're finding it tough to go it alone in tough times, read Larry's book and learn how God can be your coach."

—Rich DeVos, cofounder, Amway Corp., and owner, Orlando Magic

"Life is full of choices that are difficult to make. How do you know you're making the right decisions for you, your family, and your business? Be prepared to be encouraged and energized by GOD IS MY COACH. Through this book, Larry guides you in a way that leads to a deeper connection with God and offers clarity in the midst of confusion."

—Bob Buford, founder, Leadership Network, and author of *Halftime* and *Finishing Well*

"Larry Julian has done it again by bringing us an inspiring book of gifts in GOD IS MY COACH. In his unique, compelling writing, he shows us how we can use God's gifts to discover our authentic calling and share our gifts with others. His examples will help all of us lead fuller, more spirit-filled lives." —Bill George, author of *True North* and former CEO, Medtronic

"GOD IS MY COACH is a great resource for anyone heading into unknown territory. Whether you're seeking a new career, embarking on a new business venture or feeling stuck in your present job and desiring a change, Larry Julian's coaching process will help you face the unknown and move forward with renewed clarity, confidence, and conviction."

—Ken Melrose, former chairman and CEO, The Toro Company

"GOD IS MY COACH is a marvelous filter for the mentally fatigued. It provides a practical plan to help you cut through the clutter and chaos and allow you to focus on the meaningful."

—Brad Anderson, chairman and CEO, Best Buy Co. Inc.

GOD
IS MY
COACH

A BUSINESS LEADER'S GUIDE TO FINDING CLARITY IN AN UNCERTAIN WORLD

LARRY JULIAN

CENTER
STREET.

New York Boston Nashville

Scripture quotations are taken from the *Life Application Bible*, New International Version edition. Published jointly by Tyndale House Publishers, Inc. (Wheaton, IL) and Zondervan Publishing House (Grand Rapids, MI). Copyright 1988, 1989, 1990, 1991 by Tyndale House Publishers, Inc., Wheaton, IL 60189. All rights reserved.

Center Street
Hachette Book Group
237 Park Avenue
New York, NY 10017

Visit our Web site at www.centerstreet.com.

Center Street is a division of Hachette Book Group, Inc.
The Center Street name and logo are trademarks of Hachette Book Group, Inc.

Printed in the United States of America

First Edition: January 2009
10 9 8 7 6 5 4 3 2 1

Library of Congress Cataloging-in-Publication Data
Julian, Larry S.
    God is my coach : a business leader's guide to finding clarity in an uncertain world / Larry Julian.—1st ed.
        p. cm.
    ISBN: 978-1-59995-048-8
    1. Business—Religious aspects—Christianity. 2. Leadership—Religious aspects—Christianity.
    I. Title.
    HF5388.J85 2009
    261.8'5—dc22

                                                                    2008013719

Book design by Charles Sutherland

To the memory of my
mentor, teacher and friend
Elvin Monroe "Monty" Sholund
August 4, 1920–May 13, 2007

Thank you for revealing the wonderful God whom we serve.

CONTENTS

chapter 3

Perspective: The Gift of Appreciation / 39

chapter 4

Platform: The Gift of Your Foundation / 61

chapter 5

Power: The Gift of Pressure / 81

chapter 6

Pace: The Gift of Grace to Run Your Race / 105

chapter 7

chapter 8

ACKNOWLEDGMENTS

To my Lord Jesus Christ, thank you for being my ultimate gift in the gray.

To my family; especially my wife, Sherri, and my children, Grace and Scott, who ensure that their dad remains humble while supplying great stories of life, love, and lessons learned. Thanks also to Scott and Judy Hackett, Matt and Lolly Pisoni, Jack and Lucille Julian, Jackie and Julius Toperzer, and Steve and Lesley Hackett.

To my advisory board members, each a wise leader of character and a true brother in Christ: Dean Bachelor, Dennis Doyle, Stan Geyer, Ron James, Ken Melrose, Jim Secord, and Mike Sime.

To friends who inspire me by boldly living their faith in the business world: Jay Bennett, John Busacker, Jay Coughlan, David Frauenshuh, Jeff Hagen, Cary Humphries, Tad Piper, Jeff Siemon, and Rob Gales.

To Dan Rust for his Saturday morning insights, to Steve Waller for supplying much-needed diversions, and to Jim Walter, John Zappala, and Marty Sinacore for their lifelong friendship.

To the Village Schools of the Bible family worldwide, especially Max Frazier, who carry on the mission of Know, Grow, and Go. Thank you for sharing the story of one servant, Monty, so Jesus Christ can be revealed to many.

To Doris Sholund, a woman of great faith, who steadfastly stood behind Monty, a man of great faith, so he could serve others.

To Eric Fellman, Phil Styrlund, and the National Prayer Breakfast Business Leader Forum team, who reflect the term "Jesus plus nothing" and who've taught me how to help diverse parties meet under the Name and Person of Jesus.

To Os Hillman, Kent Humphries, and David Miller, thank you for paving the way for others to integrate their work and faith.

To the special people I've coached over the years; through my mentoring you, you've mentored me in so many ways.

To our friends Doug and Melanie Peterson, Dwight and Rhonda Schneibel, and Steve and Barb Gretch for their ongoing support and friendship.

To Rolf Zettersten, Harry Helm, Michelle Rapkin, and the Hachette Book Group team for their hard work and dedication.

To Denise Marcil and Michael Congdon for their determination and follow-through.

To the mentors on a mission who took the time to share their expertise in order to help others: Marc Belton, Dr. Jack Groppel, Dr. Os Guinness, Fred Harburg, Geoff Miller, and Rob Stevenson.

And finally, to those who've allowed their stories to be shared so others can benefit: Ward Brehm, Chris Conger, Rosalind Cook, Art Erickson, Susana Espinosa de Sygulla, Bob Fisher, Bill Hardman, Eric Pillmore, Casey Robbins, Bruce and Dayle Schnack, John Turnipseed, and Randall Zindler.

A PERSONAL LETTER TO READERS

Have you faced a dilemma where it was hard to discern the right thing to do? Have you questioned whether your actions and decisions were in alignment with God's will? Have you been in a situation where you knew what was right but that action required a risk that went against the grain of conventional wisdom? If these situations sound familiar, you've been in the gray zone.

The gray zone is the most fertile environment for success or failure. It's filled with defining moments that not only shape your character and destiny but that also impact other lives—for good or for bad. Why does one leader in the gray zone rise to the occasion while another falls victim to circumstance?

Simply, I believe that one leader chooses to discover and utilize the gifts God provides in the gray while the other chooses to go it alone. God has provided each of us with the gifts necessary to be successful in work and in life. My passion through these pages is to help you find the gifts in your gray and clarity in your chaos.

As for me, the bottom line was my god for the first thirty-seven years of my life. In 1991, I was fired. Because I had placed all my worth in what I produced, I felt worthless. In my nothingness, Jesus became the ultimate gift in the gray when He said, "Follow me."

Today, I'm in the cultivation business. I promote the growth and development of leaders through a coaching process that refines the mind, heart, and spirit. My passion is to help leaders maximize their God-given potential, and, as a result, make a difference in other people's lives.

God Is My Coach is based on biblical principles and reflects the life and teachings of Jesus Christ—the ultimate leader by example.

You may choose to accept Jesus' teaching on an intellectual level—as a model for sound business leadership—or you may choose to accept Him as the very lifeline for your learning, leadership, life, and legacy.

I invite you to join me wherever you are on your faith journey. I'm not here to judge you or convert you to my way of thinking. My role is that of a facilitator—to meet you at your point of need and introduce you to a coaching process that will help you find clarity in your uncertainty and facilitate a deeper relationship with God, your most important teacher, guide, mentor, helper, and coach.

We are each a work in progress. It's my prayer that your gray zone will become the very catalyst toward a great journey that begins today. We ask God to bless us with His wisdom, show us the gifts He's provided, and give us clarity in the chaos.

—Larry Julian

INTRODUCTION

It was a beautiful September morning. I had just completed a successful strategic planning session for the Minneapolis Convention and Visitors Bureau. Minneapolis's business, community, and government leaders had come together to create a compelling vision, identified core strategies to achieve it, and developed tangible action plans. As the session's facilitator, I took a deep breath of fall air and declared the meeting as close to "perfect" as you can get in the real world.

A mere ninety-six hours later, two planes crashed into the World Trade Center, one broke the seemingly solid barrier of the Pentagon, and another crashed into the Pennsylvania countryside. The "perfect" strategic plan was rendered useless. The clarity and vision these leaders sought and persevered to realize had become a gray fog.

In the years since, I've found that several of those leaders discovered a new sense of clarity and purpose out of the uncertainty. Not only did they rise to the occasion, they inspired others to grasp their vision. A few of the leaders, unfortunately, lost their focus. They floundered and became victims of circumstance, bringing others down with them.

What about you? How do you know you're making the right decisions when dealing with day-to-day ambiguity in your business and personal life? Are you confident you're moving in the right direction?

Most of us are talented individuals who seek God's guidance. We want to contribute to a greater purpose, make a difference, and do the right thing. Unfortunately, life is messy. We're faced with dilemmas and decisions that don't have black-and-white solutions. Rather, our circumstances are filled with unanswered questions, paradoxes, and uncertainty. I call this the *gray zone*—a time when God's Truth isn't easily discernible. While I've been conducting strategic planning for organizations for over twenty years, I've discovered that the process is terribly flawed. We've been taught to seek black-and-white solutions, minimize risk, and eliminate the gray. In reality, however, I've discovered that our true greatness as leaders lies *within* the gray.

In its simplest terms, by being willing to dwell in the gray, you have the opportunity to search out and understand how God has uniquely designed and called *you*. The resulting blessing is a series of gifts in the midst of your uncertainty. Cultivating these gifts results in clarity in your chaos and the full and abundant life God promised you. The result of your spiritual growth is spiritual reproduction: you impact lives, mentor others, and leave a legacy.

God Is My Coach is a guide for leaders who want to seek and do the right thing in the midst of uncertainty. Since I won't teach you how to rid yourself of the chaos or turn the gray zone into black and white, this approach is a radical departure from conventional wisdom. It contains no guarantees, no success formulas, and no easy solutions. Rather, I will ask you to take risks, go against the grain of logical thinking, and even challenge your beliefs. While this may not sound terribly appealing, I urge you to keep an open heart and mind. I believe that God will reward your efforts with renewed clarity and purpose. Please join with me as we find clarity and direction in an uncertain world.

A Snapshot of Today's Marketplace

Phil Styrlund, a friend and business associate, travels extensively, visiting diverse faiths and cultures. He once told me, "As I travel about the planet, I see the number-one issue is uncertainty. So many leaders are struggling to run a business in the midst of conflict, chaos, and complexity. It's like they're choking on one big ambiguity hairball!"

As the author of *God Is My CEO* and *God Is My Success*, I receive regular requests for help from business leaders who seek direction in complex and confusing circumstances. Some seek guidance to help them navigate the whitewater of rapidly changing circumstances. Some feel stuck in a quiet eddy, and they wait impatiently to hear God's call. Regardless of our situation, we each look for the assurance that we're in God's will, and we desire to move forward with a sense of confidence, courage, and conviction. Do any of these gray zones hit close to home?

❖ "The company pressures me to deliver outcomes with certainty (forecasts, sales production, revenue, etc.), yet in reality our division lives in uncertainty. How do I lead effectively in the midst of this paradox?"

❖ "I've been trying to pursue a new career but haven't found any opportunities. Will the right job come around?"

❖ "I feel called to start a workplace ministry to help employees integrate their work and faith, but still need to earn money so my son can go to college. Should I stay in my job and pursue my calling later, or should I take a leap of faith now?"

❖ "I'm retiring. I feel compelled to serve others in some way but have no idea what to do."

❖ "My business has been on a steady decline for six months in a row. I don't know how much longer I can keep it afloat. Should I continue to sink money into the business or pull the plug?"

❖ "I've been way overcommitted at work and my travel schedule keeps me away from my family. I just learned that my daughter has been battling bulimia. The next three months are make-or-break time at our division, yet

I feel compelled to be with my daughter. What should I
do?"

These dilemmas were presented by good people who want to
honor God with their lives. What mires us in the gray zone and
keeps us from discovering the clarity and courage to do the right
thing? I believe that four factors prevent us from finding God's
Truth and will:

1. Business models today demand that leaders have clarity of
   purpose, courage, and conviction. A picture of Moses (the
   Charlton Heston version, that is) powerfully leading the Is-
   raelites into the Promised Land isn't too far off. In reality,
   however, leaders often struggle alone in the gray.
2. Time demands hinder our ability to seek God's Truth. We
   live in an outcome-based society that demands immediate
   answers. Leaders are so focused on the outcome that they
   neglect the process—the process of searching for God's will.
3. Risk. Following God and doing the right thing is, at times,
   counterintuitive and countercultural. Real consequences
   such as losing a sale, receiving a demotion, being fired, and
   risking one's reputation are possible when one does the right
   thing. Consequently, leaders aren't willing to risk walking by
   faith.
4. Financial pressure clouds our judgment. In times of uncertainty, we can be so blinded by the bottom line that we don't
   allow ourselves to trust that God will provide as He promises.
   Thus, we make decisions based on our insecurity rather than
   God's promises.

The Clash of Two Worlds

In the introduction to *God Is My CEO* I describe a core issue we each face:

> While we are encouraged to follow God on Sunday, often we are not supported to make the right ethical decisions in the trenches on Monday through Friday.
>
> This paradigm has demanded that we operate in two separate worlds: a deeply personal, private, spiritual world and a very public, demanding, competitive business world. For the most part, these two worlds clash in their values, beliefs, and principles and we are caught in the middle.
>
> This separation between a true longing for meaning in the workplace and the demand to help our employers survive and thrive creates a tremendous internal dilemma. The elements of this dilemma are shown on the following chart.

Business Principles versus God's Principles	
Unwritten Business Rules	**God's Principles**
Achieve results	Serve a purpose
What can I get?	How can I give?
Success = dollars	Significance = people
Work to please people	Work to please God
Fear of the unknown	Living with hope
Leadership is being first	Leadership is being last
Take charge; surrender means defeat	Let go; surrender means victory
The end justifies the means. Get to the outcome regardless of how you accomplish it.	The means justify the end. Do the right thing regardless of the outcome.
Short-term gain	Long-term legacy
Slave to the urgent	Freedom of choice
You can never produce enough	Unconditional love

We commonly view this dilemma as an internal struggle between right and wrong. We seem to be presented with a disturbing choice: either we embrace bottom-line success and turn from God, or we accept and live by God's principles and suffer whatever negative business consequences come our way.

This either/or thinking creates great anxiety, particularly when life comes at us hard and fast. We feel trapped between the lofty ideals of God and the practical realities of daily business. Rather than responding positively to the gray, we often react in a "fight-or-flight" manner. Perhaps we fight our weaknesses and temptations, beating ourselves up when we fall short of God's ideals. Or maybe we prefer to take flight and attempt to avoid the gray altogether through denial, procrastination, rationalization, or over-analyzation.

Here's the issue: Using an either/or problem-solving process to address an ambiguous situation is ineffective. We just can't solve spiritual issues with conventional business wisdom. We hack away at surface issues but never get to the root. We're pressured to move faster and produce more, yet we're choking on a flawed strategic-thinking model. We create strategic plans to control future outcomes but have never been taught to respond effectively to the present life that is beyond our control. One thing is certain. The world is not going to stop and wait for any of us to figure out how best to deal with rapid change, complexity, and uncertainty. The world needs leaders of character who have the moral clarity and courage to do the right thing regardless of uncertainty.

God Is My Coach: A New Way to Frame the Gray

Fight-or-flight is our human response to challenging circumstances; it's an innate survival mechanism. Our human tendency to survive, however, is quite the opposite of God's plan for our lives.

When faced with uncertainty, God has designed us to respond, adapt, grow, and eventually reproduce.

A memorable *Larry King Live* program featured Dr. Robert H. Schuller and his son, the Rev. Dr. Robert A. Schuller. They were discussing uncertainty and the role God played. In rapid-fire succession, Larry King shot questions at the pastors: "Why did God allow the tsunami to kill so many people in Southeast Asia? Why did so many people have to die from Hurricane Katrina?"

The tension diffused as the younger pastor calmly responded, "Larry, the real question isn't how or why we're going to die. We're all going to die. The real question is, How are we going to live?"

Just as Larry King did, we often deal with uncertainty by demanding answers, thinking they'll bring clarity. *God Is My Coach* will take the opposite approach. Rather than demanding an answer, we will choose to live with the question. Our approach is to live, learn, and lead within the context of uncertainty, not in the absence of it. Why? Because uncertainty keeps us dependent on God. We all have an eternal hunger to search for the Truth, grow closer to God, and live a life of significance. Uncertainty is the catalyst that leads us to God. *God Is My Coach* is the means to living a significant life and to leading others in an uncertain world.

Rather than trying to eliminate uncertainty by demanding answers, let us embrace the questions of the gray. Allow the questions to unravel the uncertainties and unlock the key to greater understanding. While we may not be certain where we are going, we can be certain of the One who is leading.

The Eight Gifts in the Gray

Can you imagine not noticing a gift on the desk in front of you? Most of us can't. Ironically, though, the gifts in the gray are often missed. They're just not that obvious.

Each of the chapters that follow will present you with a question;

each question is a threshold to an unexplored territory. Questions
cause us to explore the truth and to identify where we are in relation
to the truth. A question, then, opens our hearts to a revealed truth; a
truth revealed unravels the uncertainties of our situation. The result
is a gift in the gray. The gifts you discover through this process will
make up your life plan. Think of each answer as laying down another breadcrumb—a breadcrumb that puts you on the path toward
discovery.

The Question	**The Gift**	**The Discoveries**
Chapter 1 Purpose How can I integrate my career with my calling?	The Gift of Your Unique Calling	Identify your unique gifts Discover a plan to integrate your career and calling
Chapter 2 Potential How can I fulfill my potential?	The Gift of Creativity	Learn a process for unlocking your creative potential
Chapter 3 Perspective How can I avoid becoming mired in my circumstances?	The Gift of Appreciation	Understand how to see God in your work so you can express God through your work Discover the benefits of gratitude and how to apply them
Chapter 4 Platform How do I live and communicate my faith in a diverse environment?	The Gift of Your Foundation	Discern a process to help you live and communicate your faith
Chapter 5 Power How can I keep pressure from getting the best of me?	The Gift of Pressure	Understand how you respond under pressure Discover how to transform pres- sure into power

Chapter 6 Pace How can I keep from being overwhelmed by urgent work demands?	The Gift of Grace to Run Your Race	Determine your God-given race and pace Learn how to recalibrate your pace to run your race effectively
Chapter 7 Place What's the best work environment for me?	The Gift of Your Environment	Learn how to be in the right place at the right time Find out your Environment Equation
Chapter 8 Prosperity What does it mean to live a prosperous life?	The Gift of Relationships as Your Legacy	Understand how mentoring one person determines your significance Identify the Five E's of Effective Mentorship Discover God's definition of success

Developing Your Life Plan

As you work through the eight P's, you'll gain clarity, just as pieces of a puzzle come together to create a complete picture. The chapters are interconnected like parts of a body and work together to encompass your Life Plan. At the end of this coaching process you'll have not only a clearer understanding of yourself, but also greater confidence in your decisions and direction.

To clarify, I'm not talking about traditional leadership-development training here. Leadership development focuses on developing competencies and skills rather than developing the character of the whole leader. It's a temporary patch on a deeper issue.

Both biblically and practically, the most effective change occurs when a coaching process applies to the whole person. Leadership training that focuses solely on development of a specific skill, then, falls short. In order to be a successful leader you must be a successful "whole person" or a person of "integrity." That's why we're focusing on your Life Plan—it encompasses the whole of who God made you and has called you to be.

Being a person of integrity is being a person who is complete or whole. God desires a wholehearted relationship with you. He doesn't want you to worship Him on Sunday and set Him aside Monday through Friday. Nor does He want you to be a successful leader in business and a failure as a spouse or a parent.

Assimilating these eight components separately and as a whole will help you identify your Life Plan and develop new beliefs, behaviors, and habits to achieve it. Just as a personal coach focuses on your physical health and well-being, we'll focus on your spiritual health and well-being. Being of sound spiritual health with a focus on growth will make you a better leader in *all* aspects of your life.

How to Get the Most Out of This Book

The clarity you gain through this book will come not from what you read, but by what you do with what you read. My role, then, is a facilitator. I'll help you find the clarity you seek by facilitating a deeper connection to God. We'll do this in two ways: first, by investing time alone with God, and second, by allowing yourself to be transparent and vulnerable with a select group of people who are close to you. You'll use the wisdom and encouragement you gain in the process to walk by faith in the everyday trenches of your life—the ones that are filled with uncertainty, conflicts, challenges, and chaos.

1. God Is My Coach Life Plan

But Jesus often withdrew to lonely places and prayed.

—Luke 5:16

Shortage of time is one of our biggest problems, and we are easily inundated by the busyness of life. Jesus' own use of His time provides a critical principle for effective life and leadership: Just as He often withdrew to lonely places to be with God, we need time alone with God in order to grow and be successful.

Tremendous rewards are given when we invest time alone with Him. We discover new things about God's nature, about ourselves, and principles for living a full and significant life. While God is always communicating to us, our minds are so busy that we can't hear His wisdom and teaching. Solitude and silence open doors to new revelations and spiritual growth.

This edition of *God Is My Coach* features two value-added tools. The first is the "God Is My Coach Life Plan." In this special supplement, you'll have the opportunity to work through each of the eight components and document your personal responses. Through these thought-provoking exercises, you'll discover key insights about God, yourself, and your situation and you'll practically apply what you've learned from each chapter. You'll gain the clarity that comes not from books, tapes, or lectures, but from God alone. Your finished document will become your Life Plan; the basis from which you can make future decisions.

2. God Is My Coach Discussion Guide

For where two or three come together in my name, there am I with them.

—Matthew 18:20

Regardless of group size, location, or time, you need a loving support system to help you apply your faith in daily practical life.

When you meet with another or others under the name of Jesus, you meet under the character and nature of God. Open and honest discussion about applying faith to real-life issues is an important part of your growth and development. These trusted people who love you are also gifts in the gray. They will be honest with you, will keep you accountable, and will help you on your journey. To help guide your meeting and connect you with your trusted associates, this edition includes a "God Is My Coach Discussion Guide" tool, with questions that target the most important points of each chapter.

The Passion Behind My Purpose

Since you've chosen this book, you're likely a talented individual who seeks God's guidance not only to do what is right but also to make a difference in this world. I've written this book to help people find clarity and direction in a gray and uncertain world. My purpose, however, doesn't stop there. I passionately believe that our gray circumstances are prerequisites for us to become significant leaders.

Monty Sholund, my mentor, used to say, "The significance of an event is its future" and "It doesn't matter what happens; it only matters what happens to what happens." When I was most confused and perplexed by the gray, uncertain periods in my life, Monty would offer, "Ohhhh, this is *so* valuable. Don't miss out on the privilege of your problems." I've come to treasure these great truths, however mysterious they first seemed.

There's a world of difference between a good leader and a great leader. I believe great leaders never set out to be great leaders; I believe they rise up by welcoming uncertainty, knowing it serves a purpose. With this in mind, a great leader:

❖ humbly follows so he can learn to lead;
❖ risks being vulnerable in order to reflect a power greater than herself;

❖ grows in order to grow others;
❖ is comforted in order to comfort others;
❖ is encouraged in order to be an encouragement to others; and
❖ is mentored so he can become a mentor to others.

What is your uncertainty, your chaos, your issue? I pray that you seek clarity not for your own gain, but in order to find the significance that lies within your uncertainty. Trust that God has a purpose greater than your present circumstance. Embrace your uncertainty—use it as a catalyst to seek and find the gifts God has given you.

GOD

IS MY

COACH

1

Purpose

The Gift of Your Unique Calling

Issue: How Can I Integrate My Career with My Calling?

I quietly watched as my two-year-old son worked on a wood puzzle. His body and jaw tensed as he tried to fit a piece the shape of a duck into a hole the shape of a sheep. The harder he tried, the more frustrated he became. Succumbing to frustration (as two-year-olds tend to do), he hurled the puzzle into the air and fell into a heap on the floor.

As adults, how often is this scenario played out in our careers?

The Conference Board, a leading market information company, reported in 2005 that only 50 percent of workers are satisfied with their jobs and a mere 14 percent identified themselves as very satisfied. In addition, the report states that two out of three employees don't identify with or feel motivated to drive toward their employer's business goals and objectives.[1]

Could our dissatisfaction stem at least in part from working in jobs whose skill requirements don't match our unique gifts? Are we trying to force our God-given and God-inspired uniqueness to conform to a purpose He never intended for us to have? In the end, are we ducks trying to be sheep?

Solution: Fulfill Your Unique Call with Your Unique Giftedness

For we are God's workmanship, created in Christ Jesus to do good works, which God prepared in advance for us to do.

—Ephesians 2:10

In the *Halftime Report*, Ivey Harrington Beckman tells the story of a middle-aged woman's journey to making her unique calling her life's work:

> The first time Rosalind Cook sank her hands into a mound of clay at the age of 26, her soul said, "Ah ha!"
>
> "Shaping that clay into a meaningful form was like finding a piece of myself that had been missing for a long, long time," she explains.
>
> "I realized I was trying to be who other people thought I should be, and I wasn't looking at how God created me. I reflected on what really gave me joy in life—and that was sculpting. But I still felt a bit guilty about loving it so much, until a friend watched as I pulled out my clay one evening. I cried as I said: 'I don't understand how I can have so much joy in doing this! Where's the significance? This isn't saving souls. This isn't doing anything for anyone. It just feeds me and brings me joy.'
>
> "And he replied, 'Rosalind, you are made in God's image. He's your Creator and when you use the gifts of His image that gives Him pleasure.' "[2]

When we discover our God-given design and calling and use those gifts in service to Him, we experience genuine joy and satisfaction. Giftedness is one of the clues God gives you toward discovering your calling. Exploring your giftedness helps provide clarity to your unique calling—even in the midst of your uncertainty.

Discover the Gift of Your Unique Calling

In response to the growing number of workers looking for meaning, satisfaction, and motivation, self-help books continue to flood the market. We've become a consumer-driven society looking to fulfill our needs and purpose in life. We even see God as a means to serve us. Many a prayer has started with the words *Dear God, please help me get this job.* . . . . It's about *our* satisfaction, *our* career, and *our* calling.

There's an inherent flaw in the consumer-driven approach. God created us to be *catalysts*, not *consumers*. We've been uniquely designed by God to serve *His* purpose, not *ours*. It's in discovering our true calling and then using our gifts in service to God that we experience the genuine joy and satisfaction we were seeking all along.

It may be helpful to examine how our calling became consumer-driven in the first place. Part of the blame rests in how a business views its employees. When it comes to finding the right person for the job, the business world often has it completely backwards. In my first book, *God Is My CEO*, I interviewed Horst Schulze, then CEO of Ritz-Carlton Hotels. Among his thought-provoking insights was this gem: "Our industry is notorious for getting bodies to fulfill a function—to do things. I think this is irresponsible and, in a sense, immoral. People should not just fulfill a function. They have the right to be a part of something." Rather than finding the right person with the right gifts for the right job, many organizations fall into the trap of finding bodies to fill positions.

Most of the responsibility, however, rests on us. Perhaps we seek a specific career for the wrong reasons, such as fulfilling a parent's wish, earning a target salary, meeting an organization's expectations, or trying to achieve a societal ideal. Perhaps we simply have no idea how we're uniquely gifted. Or maybe we've focused all our energy into a career but haven't taken time to discover our calling. In the end, we pursue everything but our true calling. Our jobs provide a paycheck but no sense of purpose; we make money but don't make a difference. Dissatisfaction descends upon us. We fall into a continual cycle of trying to fit into someone else's requirements rather than pursue our God-given call.

Rosalind Cook, the clay sculptor, was a teacher of the blind before becoming a stay-at-home mother of three, serving on school boards and committees. Her life was busy, and for years, sculpting terra-cotta clay was simply a hobby. And then came the day her friend explained that she brought God pleasure by using the gifts God had given her:

"From that day on I gave myself permission to sculpt. And I finally connected with its true significance in my life. I was 41. I cast my first bronze at 42 and was able to sell it almost immediately."

In the *Halftime Report*, an online publication of Halftime (an organization that teaches how those in the "halftime" of their lives can look back on what they've accomplished, understand who they are, and then redirect their time and talent for an even more purposeful second half), Ivey Beckman tells us:

Today, Rosalind's prized bronze sculptures, which range from happy, playful children to full-size images of Jesus, grace galleries throughout the world. She has donated many pieces to charities, raising far more money than any committee work she ever did. . . .

"My art is a celebration of life and its Creator," says Cook. "It gives me the opportunity to motivate people to give themselves permission to dream. If you delight in your God-given passion, He will give you the desires of your heart—because He put them there! Don't ignore what God is tugging at your heart to do; that's like saying what He has created for you isn't important. Pursue what gives you joy, and you will be amazed by the significance of what God will do through you."[3]

Your Giftedness versus Your Calling

I recently had a conversation with an individual who went into great detail about his calling. The conversation went something like: "God called me to go to . . . and then He asked me to . . . and then He asked me to . . . ." While I appreciated his passion (not to mention his energy), it sounded like God had given him a twenty-item to-do list.

When Jesus turned to His disciples and said "Follow me," He provided a considerable amount of latitude for the disciples to translate that into a calling. Each disciple used his unique life experiences, gifts, and passion to respond to Jesus' call.

My favorite definition of "calling" comes from Os Guinness, author of *The Call*. He describes it this way: "First and foremost we are called to Someone (God), not to something (such as motherhood, politics, or teaching) or somewhere (such as the inner city or Outer Mongolia)."[4]

In Dr. Guinness's definition, your calling encompasses your whole life rather than just a place or a profession. It's not doing things for God and going places for Him, but living your life through the unique set of circumstances, experiences, and giftedness He's given you.

Your unique giftedness, on the other hand, is simply how God designed you. It's the most natural way you were built to respond to life's challenges and opportunities. In essence, your unique giftedness gives you an important clue toward God's call on your life and your motivation and ability to respond to it.

The Uniqueness of Your Response

When you use your gifts in response to God's call, your work becomes a joyful form of worship. Your work is an expression of your giftedness; it's your way of working out the gifts God worked into you.

He uniquely created you to serve a purpose and then gave you a unique set of gifts to fulfill that purpose. Your calling and purpose, then, is different from your brother's calling, your mother's purpose, and your best friend's calling.

The call is in God's hands. The response is in your hands. God didn't create you to be a puppet that would do His will, nor did He dole you out an assignment. Instead, He gives you great latitude to respond to your unique call. In essence, God's calling is His purpose for your life, and your response (the discovery and utilization of your unique gifts) is part of your purpose for your life. When His purpose aligns with your purpose, your work becomes a joyful and significant journey.

Rosalind Cook pulled away from her community work and reflected on what really gave her joy in life: her sculpting. When word of her talent spread, the requests for commissioned work became overwhelming.

"I asked the Lord for the strength to say no to some requests because I wanted everything I did to have real significance—value other than a pretty piece of bronze to sell in a gallery."

Ivey Beckman describes Rosalind's epiphany:

> Soon afterward Rosalind did a small head study of a woman with a turban draped over one shoulder. The sculpture stopped at the clavicle.
>
> "I wanted to create a woman who depicted beauty not because of her hair, not because of her body, but because she had this inner strength and dignity," explains Rosalind.
>
> Weeks later a friend saw the small piece in Rosalind's studio and asked if she would donate it as a fundraiser for Tulsa Project Woman, an organization that helps women who have no health insurance pay for breast cancer treatments.
>
> "I finished the piece and took it to my foundry to have my mold done and asked for Suzy, who always does them for me. But Suzy wasn't there," Rosalind recalls. "I learned she had breast cancer and

was taking chemo treatments. In tears, I told her coworkers what the sculpture was for and was astounded to learn that Project Tulsa Woman had paid for Suzy's treatment."

Later Rosalind asked Suzy to speak at the event in which the small bronze sculpture would be unveiled. Although shy, Suzy bravely told a crowded room how Tulsa Project Woman took her death sentence and gave her the gift of hope.

"Everyone there was in tears as Suzy, who had lost her hair and her breast, stood beside the sculpture of a woman who depicted beauty—not because of her hair, not because of her body, but because she had inner strength and dignity," recalls Rosalind. "Suzy was the living embodiment of that sculpture, and the money to help more women poured in. God honored my prayer for significance by taking the least significant thing I had done and making it the most significant. His hands guided mine to shape that small study because He knew exactly what His purpose was."[5]

Understanding Your Giftedness: The Motivated Abilities Pattern (MAP®)

In January 2003, Rob Stevenson, managing director of People Management International, a firm that specializes in executive searches, executive coaching, and organizational effectiveness, introduced me to a whole new way of becoming what God designed me to be: the Motivated Abilities Pattern® (MAP®) developed through the SIMA® (System for Identifying Motivated Abilities®) discovery process.

Arthur Miller, the founder of People Management, distilled his years of research into this insightful discovery: "The surest way I have found to unlock the essence of a person is to look at what he likes to do and does well."[6] The simplicity is beautiful. Your giftedness is the intersection of what you naturally do well with what you love doing.

The MAP® is the system People Management developed to identify and describe a person's unique giftedness. They found that all patterns of giftedness have five dimensions:

1. Abilities The abilities you love to use. These are the natural strengths and competencies you employ to accomplish the results you want (i.e., study, experiment, analyze, persuade, strategize, teach, etc.).

2. Subject Matter The things you love to work with; the objects or subject areas to which you're naturally drawn and in which you achieve your most productive and fulfilling achievements (i.e., numbers, concepts, people, tools, machines, color, etc.).

3. Circumstances The ideal environment; situations or settings that stimulate you to achieve. These are the ideal conditions in which you function (i.e., structured, visible, competitive circumstances, etc.) and the factors that "trigger" your motivation (i.e., needs, problems, potential for measurable results, etc.).

4. Operating Relationships The way you interact with others in order to accomplish meaningful results (i.e., team member, individualist, spark plug, facilitator, coordinator, etc.).

5. Payoff The outcome or goal you love to work toward in order to feel a sense of accomplishment and satisfaction (i.e., excel, overcome, meet requirements, gain response, acquire goods and status, pioneer, etc.).[7]

The MAP® process encompasses your whole life, not just one segment of your life. Your giftedness is not just about finding your strengths but about finding your passion, your circumstances, your relationships, and the meaning and satisfaction you seek. When we integrate all five areas of our giftedness into a whole, we get a better sense of how God designed us to achieve our calling.

In the "God Is My Coach Life Plan," we'll go through an abbreviated MAP® process to help you discover your unique giftedness. You'll discover gifts you never realized you had.

Mentor on a Mission

Robert J. Stevenson, managing director of People Management International, is a nationally known management consultant in senior management selection, organizational design and development, executive coaching, succession planning, and workplace change and innovation. Rob was excited to be able to give some practical ideas about this topic—our unique giftedness, purpose, and calling—in order to bring it within our grasp.

Q: What is the greatest misperception about gifts?

A: Most people suffer under the delusion that the gifted and talented make up less than 5 percent of the population. That's wrong. One hundred percent of us are gifted and talented.

Q: What frustration do you experience working with clients?

A: We see many people who are gifted but disengaged because they're doing the wrong job for the wrong reason. Their gifts have been squelched and discouraged by well-meaning but misdirected helpers, counselors, teachers, and friends.

Q: What is the most important point you would like to make about giftedness?

A: God has placed in you a defined and refined system of giftedness that has functioned seamlessly since you were born. You are uniquely gifted; therefore, no standardized test can describe your uniqueness. The answer lies within you. The repeating pattern of your giftedness lies within the stories that reveal what you enjoy doing and do well, your "sweet spot."

Q: How can I communicate my unique giftedness in a job interview?

A: First, you need to explore and know your "sweet spot"—that special area where your passion and purpose shine. You can't sell a product until you understand its unique benefits to the customer. In the same way, you can't sell yourself until you know what you enjoy doing and do well. There's no unemployment for a person who knows his or her gifts well enough to communicate and leverage them.

Second, your value to an employer or organization is based on three areas: 1) your professional experience, 2) your education or training, and, finally, and most importantly, 3) your unique giftedness. You need to integrate all three areas to tell your story effectively.

Counsel for Consideration

When you're dwelling in a time period that's gray and filled with chaos, it's easy to grow impatient with your circumstances. Like my son, Scott, with his puzzle, we try to force the shape of a duck into an opening meant for a sheep. *Don't force your God-given and God-inspired uniqueness to conform to a purpose He never intended for you to have.* Instead of seeking external clarity and direction, focus your efforts on the internal to find your genuine calling.

There are resources and organizations that can help you find your strengths, personality type, and gifts. I chose to share People Management's process for three reasons:

1. The process analyzes stories from your entire life, not just one time period. Imbedded within your life story is a treasure chest of clues to your calling. Your giftedness isn't just about finding your strengths; it's also about your passion, your best circumstances, your relationships, and the meaning and satisfaction you seek. Allow the process to help you discover how these five dimensions bring out the best in you so you can bring out the best in those around you.
2. God has provided clues to your giftedness since you were born. Taking time to identify your most satisfying moments from your past and then fleshing out these stories is an invaluable tool. The process itself is an important exercise in discovering how God uniquely designed you.
3. Putting the pieces of your giftedness together is like putting together a jigsaw puzzle. It can be a frustrating, pressure-filled task of trying to force the duck piece into the sheep-shaped hole or, if you're patient, it can be a fascinating journey from gray to clarity.

Going through this process won't, on its own, provide you with clarity of purpose and direction. Further, it would be misleading to tell you that simply doing what you love will help you discover your career and calling. There are times, for example, when circumstances dictate that you must provide for your family, even though you may not love what you're doing. Discovering your giftedness is one of the many clues God provides. Ultimately, we must trust that God has us in the gray for a reason. Seeking God's call and discovering how to use your gifts in service to God and others is a noble pursuit. Trust in the process and trust in God. He will provide the clarity and calling you seek in His perfect timing.

2

Potential

The Gift of Creativity

Issue: How Can I Fulfill My Potential?

I t was finals week at Michigan State. My college housemate, Bob, poked his head into my room and said, "Hey, let's play some basketball!" In desperate need of a study break, I joined him.

Bob was one of those "all-American, most likely to succeed" guys, gifted in everything from sports to academia. Catching up to Bob outside, I saw that he was high. In addition to his bloodshot eyes, he was unusually energetic. We arrived at the court to find two guys, the shorter of whom looked to be six-foot-seven, practicing free throws. Bob challenged them to a game.

Turning in dumbfounded amazement, I protested, "What are you, nuts? I'm five-eight and have the leaping ability of a cow." Bob replied, "Don't worry, just feed me the ball and let me do the rest." I watched as Bob ran circles around the two giants.

When I came back from my final that afternoon, I found Bob lying on the couch, drunk. "How did your finals go?" I asked. "Didn't go," he responded. "It was just too much research. Plus, I'm not creative." Bob went on to rationalize that since he had a decent job waiting for him regardless, there was really no reason to graduate and approach an uncertain world.

We're gifted with unlimited potential, yet when confronted with the unknown, our fears and egos make our gray zone even murkier. Faced with thoughts like *I'm not creative*, *I can't risk it*, *It's impractical*, or *It's impossible*, we wonder, How can I fulfill my potential?

Solution: Take Creative Charge of Your God-Given Purpose

With man this is impossible, but with God all things are possible.
—Matthew 19:26

Art Erickson, CEO of Urban Ventures, tackles the impossible. His inspiration is an inner-city community in South Minneapolis known as "Crack Alley," an area abandoned by the affluent, isolated by interstates, and decimated by drugs.

"I remember reading about George Washington Carver," Art explains. "Upon graduating from Iowa State Agricultural College, he prayed, 'Lord, I've prepared myself for your best; now give me your best.' Carver was expecting presidencies and leadership roles. Instead, God gave him a peanut, saying, 'George, take my peanut, find out all you can about it and develop it.' In the years that followed, Carver fostered soil development, improved it by crop rotation, and discovered more than 300 uses for the peanut, including dyes, soaps, wood stains, plastics, synthetic rubber, and other products. By the time he died in 1943, Carver's efforts had altered the economy of the South.

"I see a two-by-five-block focus territory and a radius mile impact area containing 46,000 people, 13,000 of whom are children under the age of eighteen, as my peanut. My success isn't about personal upward mobility or exponential expansion. It's about developing everything I can out of the peanut God gave me."

What's your peanut? Rather than wait for creative inspiration, put your gifts to work right now on the peanut you've been given. Accept the blessing that comes in the form of the uncertain, the improbable, and the impossible. Your uncertainty is the door to your destiny; your creativity is the key to unlocking your potential.

Discover the Gift of Creativity

I grieve when talented, gifted people fall short of their God-given potential. More often than not, I believe our own ego, fears, and self-limiting thoughts get in the way of our creativity, even though God has blessed us with unlimited creative potential.

God created us in *His* image: He designed us to be creators. Just for a moment, look around and marvel at what humans have created—cities with skyscrapers, inspiring art and music, life-changing books, systems that govern nations, space exploration, medical advances that have doubled life expectancies, wide-ranging technology, and ever-expanding ways to communicate with each other.

Perhaps you're saying, "Gee whiz, I'm not looking to change the world, I'm just looking for some clarity and direction." I understand, but bear with me.

Our limiting thoughts keep us impoverished by the impossible, but Scripture tells us that with God all things are possible. Creativity is the pursuit of the possible. It's a practical gift given to each and every one of us. In fact, we've each been called to be His creative stewards on earth. We're uniquely called to use our God-given gifts to build, create, restore, develop, and even make something out of nothing. At our core, we've been given the ability to transform chaos into clarity, problems into opportunities, and the impossible into the possible.

As I waited to talk to Art Erickson, I reflected on the uncomfortable drive from my home in the suburbs. I drove from tree-lined neighborhoods of innocent children waiting for yellow school buses on quiet street corners to drug dealers waiting for buyers, the street corners marked by graffiti. *Why would anyone choose to tackle this problem?* I thought. *Talk about impossible.*

Rushing in, Art apologized, saying, "Sorry I'm late! Our garage was broken into last night. They cleared out everything."

He ushered me into a conference room with an aerial view of

South Minneapolis. Like a field general looking over a battlefield, Art described every square foot of his small community. The community calls the area Crack Alley and the Alexander Brothers Porn Empire, but Art calls it the Oz, or Opportunity Zone.

Where others see the impossible, Art has strategically implemented the possible. No matter how impossible the problem, a corresponding vision has instilled healing and hope. Art deeply understands the issues and has developed creative solutions. Where there was rampant unemployment, Art started job programs. Where there were gangs, he implemented youth programs. Where absentee fathers had decimated family life, Urban Ventures began marriage and fathering programs.

Art doesn't consider himself a creative or innovative thinker, but rather the creative steward of the gifts and resources God has given to the community. He's the promoter of possibilities, the developer of dreams, and the restorer of hope for community families and businesses.

"You're a smart leader with many gifts," I said. "You could be working at a nice job in an area where your house would be safe. What inspires you to do this job in the midst of such adversity and uncertainty?"

"Because," Art explained, *"this is my peanut."*

Think about your own situation. Is it possible that God has already gifted you with your peanut? Rather than wait for creative inspiration, put your gifts to work right now on the peanut you've been given. Choose not to be enslaved by your ego or stymied by your self-centeredness and accept the blessing that comes in the form of uncertainties, impracticalities, and impossibilities.

The Seven Keys to Unlocking Your Creative Potential

1. Invest

When Sherri and I were married, we each brought a dog into our new life together. Zack, a golden retriever, had been as loyal and steadfast a companion to me as Tovah, a German shepherd, had been to my wife. The dogs fought as they tried to adjust to a new life together and both began to behave differently. We hired a dog behaviorist to give us some recommendations.

The dog expert came to our house to observe us. Zack, now twelve years old, lay comfortably by the fireplace. I was several feet away with Sherri and Tovah. I had just given Tovah a treat and called Zack to come for his. Despite my repetition, the old dog just stared at me. I turned to the dog expert and asked, "That dog has been coming for treats for twelve years and now he just lies there. What's wrong with him?" Laughing, the dog expert replied, "Cost-benefit analysis. Zack is thinking, 'What's it going to cost me to raise these old tired bones from this warm fire, to deal with that crazy dog, just for a treat?'" The cost was simply too high for the reward, so he played it safe and did nothing.

Investment is defined as putting resources (money, time, or talent) to use in order to gain a profitable return. The conventional business wisdom for decision making is the cost-benefit analysis. Simply defined, we weigh the cost of an investment against the potential benefit to ensure that the perceived benefit outweighs the cost.

In times of uncertainty, conventional wisdom teaches us to play it safe and minimize the risk. We naturally hold back on investing in new ventures or projects, or even in the "peanut" God's given us.

God, however, calls us to invest our time, talents, and resources toward fulfilling our God-given potential, even in times of uncertainty. In God's economy, uncertainty isn't a cost but a *catalyst* for creating a better future.

God implores us to make investments in our creative potential. Compelling evidence of this is found in the Parable of the Loaned Money (Matthew 25): To the one who used his talents wisely, God responded, "Well done, good and faithful servant! . . . Come and share your master's happiness!" To the one who buried his talents because he was afraid, God responded, "You wicked, lazy servant! . . . Take the talent from him and give it to the one who has the ten talents."

I had difficulty understanding why Art Erickson would invest in a house in a neighborhood riddled with problems. I, of course, used the cost-benefit approach. Art, on the other hand, considered the benefit to be more important than the cost. He understood both the peanut he'd been given and how his leadership could benefit the community.

"Why," I asked, "would you live in the inner city when others are leaving for a better life?" Decisively, he responded, "I'm called to be a reflection of Jesus Christ. Jesus totally emptied Himself in service to others. He invested His entire life toward the healing, reconciliation, and restoration of people within His community. I need to do the same."

Investing is the first key to unlocking your creative potential. Don't ask what it will cost; ask what you're willing to invest in order to fulfill your creative potential.

2. Investigate

In times of uncertainty, we often try to solve our problems quickly. We think, *I hate my job; I need to find a new one* or *We're losing out to the competition; we've got to capture more market share.* This thinking clouds our gray circumstances even further. Like a horse wearing blinders, we investigate solutions from a limited viewpoint. Perhaps we investigate job opportunities that fit our needs without considering how we can fulfill the needs of a prospective employer, or we investigate how to make our business more profitable without thinking about how the customer would profit from our future strategies. In short, our thinking is self-centered.

When we view our circumstances through God's eyes, life becomes an exciting exploration. Rather than focus inward on our problems, we focus outward on the world. As Henry Blackaby states in *Experiencing God*, "Watch to see where God is working and join Him!"[1]

In the Investigation stage, our goal is to observe our surroundings, discover where God is working, and join in. We do this through deliberate efforts of observing, listening to others, determining the market of people you want to help, and researching the underlying challenges your market faces. Investigation is important because it provides the groundwork for putting your creative potential to work.

Giving me a tour of his neighborhood, Art Erickson pointed out things I simply hadn't seen, from prostitution to drug deals. He recognized every suspicious trouble spot and every safe haven of hope. He knew every person on the street. I never heard Art pass judgment on a person; instead, he discerned opportunities to serve. Whether looking at a saint or a sinner, he asked the same questions: *What's the biggest problem you're facing? Tell me more about your situation. What do you need to make the situation better?*

Quoting his friend Tom Skinner, Art tells me, "Before I can understand the good news, I must understand the bad news." Summarizing his approach, he said, "The needs, pain, issues, and problems of the people in my community have been the catalysts for ideas and creative solutions."

Art isn't a distant observer; he's a detective looking for clues in order to apply creative solutions. The same principle applies to you. In the midst of uncertainty, investigate the needs of others and you'll begin to unlock your creative potential.

3. Illuminate

To illuminate is to enlighten spiritually. It's the point where something becomes clear. While we often think of this as a flash of clarity, such as when the Apostle Paul met Jesus on the road to Damascus, more often than not our inspiration comes in a series of small revelations. Rather than experiencing the vista from a mountaintop on a clear day, we receive glimpses of God in the gray and difficult dilemmas of everyday life. It's as if these enlightened thoughts, ideas, insights, and inspirations are little breadcrumbs from God to guide us in our journey. One revelation leads to another, which leads to another, and we're soon moving down a new path.

The goal of this stage is to be aware of and capture each of these revelations. Together, they begin to bring clarity to your gray circumstances.

My friend Jay Bennett compares illumination to a rheostat—an adjustable light switch. The more you turn the dial by investing yourself in the creative process through service and compassion for others, the more illumination you gain. Jay describes illumination as "those moments of revelation when I get bits of truth that are relevant to my particular circumstances. It happens sometimes when I pray. Or it happens when I'm reading the Bible in pursuit of seeking answers to life's issues. It happens when I'm with others and it happens when I'm alone in His presence. Thoughts just pass through my mind, words are processed in my heart, and sometimes I can see what God wants me to see."

Art Erickson believes, "Illumination grows out of a need. I've always had a heart for kids because that's where the greatest potential for community transformation lies. They're the most in need and they're the most open. So my strategy has always been to look for ideas to reach the unreached. Many of our ideas were born out of talking to kids in the lunchroom. I would deliberately have lunch with kids in the elementary, middle, and high schools. They would ask questions and I would ask questions. I discovered they had no recreation area so I developed an idea to find a gym and create a basketball league. In the summer, we discovered there was nothing in the city for kids to do. That eventually transformed into 72 summer programs with 55 staff and 1,600 kids. A church pastor lamented that kids never go to church. We came up with an idea to bring church to them. We created a music festival. Twenty years later, the Soul Liberation Festival continued to grow with over 20,000 people in attendance over an 8-day period.

"It all starts with a need," Art explains. "I get an idea on how to respond to the need and as I act upon the idea, things start to develop."

Unleash your creative potential through illumination, the ability to capture these random thoughts, ideas, insights, and revelations as a means for exploring clues toward a greater vision.

4. Imagine

Illumination inspires your imagination. The random thoughts, ideas, and insights you've been collecting begin to work together to create an image in your mind. Imagination is the power to form an image of something not yet present. It's at this stage that we begin to envision what can be versus what is. We start to envision the possible rather than remain mired in the impossible. Our vision is brought into light.

How are we supposed to create a God-inspired vision of the future and begin to fulfill it while in the midst of a gray and uncertain world that demands answers now? Start walking in the light of the vision and trust that the clarity of the vision will reveal itself in its proper time. Oswald Chambers says, "Every God-given vision will become real if we will only have patience."

The reality is that we often don't have a clear vision of the future, *nor are we supposed to.* We grow impatient because we believe we must have a complete vision and plan before starting something. As a result, we do nothing (play it safe) or we do something (run ahead of God with our own vision). Both approaches lead to frustration and futility.

When driving from Phoenix to Las Vegas, for example, you first see nothing but desert. Eventually, a hazy mountain range appears in the distance. The closer you get, the clearer things become. It's not until many miles elapse that you experience the mountain scene filled with detail, color, and rich perspectives.

In the same way, God gives us a vision for the future, but He isn't always ready to reveal it in full. Our first glimpses of the vision are hazy and unclear. Maybe we're not yet ready to see it. Maybe we're not yet prepared to fulfill it. Or maybe we need to grow in character in order to handle it.

1 Corinthians 2:9 promises us, *No eye has seen, no ear has heard, no mind has conceived what God has prepared for those who love him.* Sometimes we need to trust in what we don't see and believe in what we can't conceive. Imagination allows us to trust that God's vision lies ahead though we see nothing today. Imagination allows us to trust in God's unseen possibilities rather than in our self-imposed limited vision. As Frank Gaines said, "Only he who can see the invisible can do the impossible."

Sometimes we imagine something so big, so spectacular, and so significant that it frightens us. We dismiss the vision by claiming we can't do it or it's impossible. Our only real choice is to accept the vision and know that if it's of God, it will grow and clarify over time. If it isn't, it will eventually die away.

Art Erickson's vision was to raise up a new generation of kids as the primary means to restore the inner-city community. He created strategies to develop kids educationally, technically, and vocationally, but morally, the issue was deep and complex.

Perhaps the toughest issue facing the inner city today is fatherlessness. A report Art received was both startling and sobering: 80 percent of kids didn't live in the same home as their birth father. Art pondered the toughest of the toughest dilemmas, asking, "How will we impact these fathers so they can impact their kids?"

Art knew that an Ozzie-and-Harriet vision of an inner-city family would be deflating and insulting. "I know one kid who became the father of twenty-three children before he graduated high school," he explained. "It was a badge of honor." The issue includes a multitude of spiritual, cultural, societal, and economic factors. Where do you start? How do you create and fulfill a vision when you are mired in such a complex, ambiguous, and uncertain dilemma? One victory at a time.

Art started with one question: How do we put marriage back into the neighborhood? With that in mind, he and his wife, Kathy, created a Marriage Weekend. Twenty couples attended. Art required that the couple be married. If a man and woman were living together and not married, they could come for the daytime meetings, but couldn't stay overnight.

Two days after the marriage conference, Jeremy, an eighth-grade boy, came to shovel Art's driveway following a snowstorm. Jeremy asked, "You just got back from the marriage conference, didn't you? Jane and Jason were there, weren't they?" Jason was Jeremy's mentor and had been married shortly before the conference. Then Jeremy exclaimed, "If I gave my girlfriend a ring, could we go to the next Marriage Growth Weekend?"

"There's a new story to tell in the neighborhood," Art explains. He went on to say that Jeremy, like 80 percent of his peers, had never experienced the concept of marriage. Now there is at least one boy who has a seed of an idea that has the potential to grow and spread.

If you're in the midst of a gray and complex situation, you don't need a vision plaque for your wall. Implement one idea at a time. Step out in your faith and allow the vision to become clear in God's perfect timing.

5. Incubate

To incubate means to allow ideas or insights to become internalized deep within your soul. Your imagination kicks into high gear and ideas and insights begin to gel into tangible visions, ideas, and plans. It's a critical time to nurture and grow your vision. In a miraculous process, these tiny seeds of thoughts begin to form the basis of a very tangible creation. Perhaps this represents a new business venture or an innovative way to integrate your career and your calling. Regardless of what the creation is, there's a critical time period where not only does the idea need to grow, but you also need to grow in order to give birth to the idea.

Ideas and businesses often fail because the venture was impatiently begun prior to fully developing the idea. Neither the idea nor the champion of the idea was properly prepared for the plan's realities and challenges.

Urban Ventures' programs have developed through a slow process of incubating and implementing ideas over forty years. It all started with the question, How do we reach the unreached? Art explains, "I'm a garbage can. I collect everything. I get an idea on how to reach some kid and I toss it in the can. Somehow, when the opportunity is right, I can pull out the idea and act on it."

Allow your ideas to incubate until they've become tangible visions and plans. At the same time, allow God the time He needs to prepare you to champion the plan (and the peanut) He's given you.

6. Innovate

Innovation is taking an idea and converting it into a practical application. This is the stage where a conceptual idea or vision is transformed into a viable product, service, or plan. Perhaps a new business venture is developed, an old business is retooled, or a career is enhanced. This phase is much more perspiration than inspiration; it requires hard work, discipline, and perseverance. Innovation requires the communication skills of an ambassador and the determination of a bulldog.

Your creative potential is tested at every stage, but the innovation stage will provide you with one of your greatest tests. You've invested time, talent, and energy, but have yet to transform your vision into a practical reality or a viable business. Ironically, with each level of creative growth you'll find that a new gray zone confronts you. As my friend Jay Bennett describes it, "New level, new devil!"

Stay focused on the process, not the outcome. If God has brought you to this point, He will guide you through your present challenge.

Take a step back and remember that you've been uniquely designed to accomplish God's work. We (and our creative ventures) will be works in progress until the day we die. Continue to incubate your vision, working out of love and with your hope placed in Him. Hold on to His promise that *No eye has seen, no ear has heard, no mind has conceived what God has prepared for those who love him.*

As you've seen, one of Art Erickson's leadership talents is his ability to take a spiritual vision and apply innovation until it becomes a tangible and practical service or solution. Art understands that the vision of restoring communities by developing youth and families isn't his; he's the creative steward of God's vision. Art is more of a storyteller than a salesperson. He doesn't sell his vision; he allows others to connect with God's vision. Art explains, "People connect with the vision of redeeming and building a new culture around God's original values—the values of grace, love, reconciliation, forgiveness, and families."

Urban decay is both a spiritual and an economic problem. Since the issue falls through the cracks of business, government, and church communities, Art "connects the dots." As the creative steward of the vision, Art's job is to marshal the hearts and the resources of business, church, and government to solve the issue of urban decay. He's highly effective at building strategic partnerships that connect the ideals of a compelling vision with practical benefits and solutions.

That's your challenge, too. *God gave you a peanut.* The peanut has incubated into a vision and God has given you the role of creative steward of His vision. Your success now is based on how you bring the vision to the marketplace, on how you connect the dots. Expect it to be difficult and require your hard work and perseverance. Work it until it becomes a tangible and practical service or solution, and then use your innovation to connect others to a vision greater than yourself.

7. Improvise

Improvisation is the art of responding in the moment to one's surroundings. It's the ability to create or invent something out of nothing, without prior preparation. This final stage of the creative process is the flashpoint where creativity, risk, and the unknown intersect with the present realities of daily life. Planning and preparation are crucial, but sometimes life comes down to adapting to the present. While we do all we can to prepare for the uncertainties of life, when faced with the unknown, we often don't know how to improvise.

I watched as a political candidate began to give an important speech on CNN. She was reading a carefully crafted speech when one of the pages wafted to the ground. The candidate was rendered speechless. She was so focused on what she'd prepared that she had no capacity to respond to an unplanned moment.

Conversely, there's Robin Williams. Asked a specific question in a late-night interview, he responds with several rapid-fire and divergent thoughts. While Robin Williams is brilliant, he's also learned the art of improvisation.

As a business leader, you can learn to improvise in very practical terms. I occasionally find myself in situations that are fraught with hidden political agendas. As much as I prepare in advance, I find myself losing control as a discussion heads down a path of conflict. Improvisation helps me think quickly when conversations begin to head south, and I'm able to steer the discussion back on course.

The inner city is all too often the site of horrendous acts that reveal the worst of society. It requires that we respond. Some choose not to see this, some observe from a distance, and some react in anger. Improvisation is how you respond when an ideal vision of the future and a present reality clash. Art Erickson intuitively uses improvisation in his work, such as when a senseless community tragedy occurs.

"There was a vigil on Sunday for Earnell Luster," Art begins. "He tried to save two women who were being beaten by gang members. They kicked Earnell into unconsciousness and left him for dead. Then they took his shoes as trophies. A gang act of defiance and triumph. Over a hundred people gathered to mourn, pray for peace, speak against violence, and celebrate Earnell's life.

"Improvisations are ideas and inspirations that come from God at the right time He wants to give them. Every challenge becomes an opportunity to live and fulfill our vision," he concludes.

How does Art live in the light of a vision of hope when he's confronted with the darkness of violence every day? He improvises. He creates something out of nothing. He provides hope in the midst of hopelessness, love in response to hate, and reconciliation in the midst of violence.

Our challenges may not be as harsh as those faced by Art and his community, but they are challenges nonetheless. How can you improvise when you're met with opposition? How can you respond to daily challenges and obstacles?

Improvisation is where your creative potential comes alive as you respond to life's daily challenges. Remember, God is in the gray. As Josh Billings wrote, "Life is a grindstone. Whether it grinds you down or polishes you up depends on the stuff you're made of."

Do you know how the words you're reading were written and

edited? Through improvisation. As in many marriages, God blessed my wife and me with complementary skills. I write. My wife edits. She's also a full-time mom and the heartbeat of our home. In order to get this book edited, we've had to improvise. I've logged more miles behind a stroller, visited more playgrounds, and swum in more pools than I ever thought possible. While I might have preferred to meet with a few more people over some leisurely lunches, sometimes you've just got to improvise.

Trust that God has given you the creative ability to respond to whatever life throws at you. One of the main messages of improvisation is to lighten up. Even with its pressures and challenges, life can be fun. Rather than seeing the challenges of the day as a daily grind, choose to accept this day as a joyful adventure.

Mentor on a Mission

Marc Belton is the executive vice president of Worldwide Health, Brand, and New Business Development for General Mills, Inc. Marc has invested his creative efforts in his business career and in roles in several community organizations. He sat down with me to talk about the importance of creativity in business.

Q: What are the greatest challenges to applying one's God-given creativity in business?

A: The greatest challenge is the belief that you're not creative enough. It's the kiss of death. This belief is driven by two things: lack of confidence and pride. The worst is pride because it's a preoccupation with self. It creates an inherent fear of being wrong, being seen as different, or saying something stupid.

Q: How do you apply your God-given creativity at General Mills?

A: First, I realize that when I walk through that door to work, I'm not bringing myself; I'm bringing the spirit of wisdom and the presence of God to the workplace. He's the author of wisdom and inspiration. Recognizing the true source of this wisdom is the key to being a creative and innovative leader. It's about walking with a level of confidence and trust that His spirit works in me at all times.

Second, it's more important to see others as His created children who have been uniquely gifted with creative skills and talents. We live in an individualistic society that says it's about us: scoring the touchdown, bringing the creative ideas to the table, doing it all. The most creative people are working in teams. Nobody is as smart as everybody. Nobody is as creative as everyone. My role as a leader is to bring out the best in the people around me. My prayer is, "God, help me help the people around me to discover their gifts and apply them to solve different problems."

I don't get into "It's my gig; I have to bring the ideas because I'm the top guy" or "They're expecting me to have all the answers and ideas." The truth of the matter is I'm not expecting to have any of those things, but I sure am expecting me to be in a position to learn how to bring out the best in others so these great ideas can surface. Then, collectively, we can make them happen.

Q: What advice can you give leaders to help them unleash the creative potential with their respective organizations?

A: The key is to create an environment and culture of innovation and creativity. First, you need to create a spirit of openness. We need to be open to all ideas. Second, develop an attitude of creativity. All problems can be solved (with the help of God). Next is an attitude—big aspirations foster big creativity, small goals foster incrementalism. Next is immersion—getting our people to live the lives of the consumers for whom they're innovating. Really observe, listen, and look for ways to solve the problems for the consumers we serve. Next is stimulation—bringing ideas from different areas, learnings, and disciplines and using them to stimulate our group. Next is collaboration—none of us is as smart or creative as all of us. Finally, persistence—there's always a level of tenacity involved with doing anything creative. You have to be like a dog on a bone; you have to stay on it.

Q: Risk is a big part of creativity. What advice can you share about risk?

A: There are always risks. The biggest risk is doing nothing in a competitive and dynamic marketplace. We undervalue the risk of doing nothing and staying with the status quo. Oftentimes, the marketplace is changing right in front of you. If you aren't willing to take the risk, then you may find yourself in another's rearview mirror two years later.

Q: What advice can you give readers to apply their God-given creativity at work?

A: Get past your ego and pride and allow God to use you. Ask

Him to help you bring out the best in others. Every day I come to work, I pray, "Lord, bring out the best in me today. Help me get over me so I can be useful to others." We serve a God who can empower us to be more than we can be on our own. Think and pray about that as you come to work.

Counsel for Consideration

If people knew how hard I worked to get to my mastery, it wouldn't seem wonderful at all.

—Michelangelo

American Idol provides an insightful look into the culture of today's youth. Thousands upon thousands of young adults audition to become the next vocal star. Particularly fascinating is the response of those who are rejected. While some accept constructive criticism, others react in disbelief and anger. They seem to carry an expectation that a star is simply born; that there is no need to work at one's creative potential. Somehow, we've created a sense of entitlement coinciding with a need for immediate gratification.

Compare the egos of these *American Idol* contestants to Bob, my Michigan State friend who chose not to go for his dream because he felt he wasn't creative. Ironically, both have the same self-centered view. Whether it's displayed as the "I'm a star!" scream of an ego or the "I'm not creative" whisper of fear and insecurity, self-centeredness keeps us from unlocking our God-given potential.

Art Erickson uses his creativity to unlock potential and provide clarity where there is uncertainty. George Washington Carver wanted to use his talents to be a leader among leaders. Instead, God gave him a peanut and said, "George, do all you can with this peanut." Art Erickson could have been a highly paid corporate executive, yet he humbly chose to work with his peanut. He also chose to tackle the impossible. In forty years, Art's work has changed countless lives and made a significant difference in the community, not by leading from the mountaintop but by working on his peanut in the trenches of difficult circumstances, day in and day out.

Unlocking and unleashing your creative potential is a lifelong pursuit. Whether looking for a new career, starting a new business, or entering a new stage in life, trust that God has given you every gift in order to be the successful and significant person He designed you to be. Take creative charge of your God-given purpose and remember God's promise to you in 1 Corinthians 2:9: *No eye has seen, no ear has heard, no mind has conceived what God has prepared for those who love him.*

3

Perspective

The Gift of Appreciation

Issue: How Can I Avoid Becoming Mired in My Circumstances?

Challenging short-term circumstances were sending the owner and her successful business spinning out of control. Three months of falling short of revenue projections led to a tornado of issues that overwhelmed her ability to run her business effectively. Upon analysis, though, we found that the business downturn wasn't related to any major organizational flaws, nor was it related to any particular competition or downward trends in the marketplace. It was simply a set of order cancellations coupled with a temporary delay in business from a key account.

Unfortunately, the owner didn't see it that way. She started to panic. With each passing month, she grew increasingly anxious about the company's future. Over and over, she asked, "How can this happen to *my* business?"

In her panic, she alienated and even abused her loyal employees. She forced some who had been with the company for twenty years into early retirement and eventually fired the sales director and his team. She even took it out on her own family, alienating her two daughters and leaving her husband.

This woman had a successful business, good health, and a loving family, yet she allowed a set of circumstances to be her downfall. In the end, it really wasn't her circumstances that did her in—it was her perspective.

How can we avoid becoming mired in the tangible? When challenges and uncertainties threaten to overwhelm us, what can we do? Is there another perspective?

Solution: Trust in the Unseen

Now faith is being sure of what we hope for and certain of what we do not see.

—Hebrews 11:1

Susana Espinosa de Sygulla was a young business owner who was financially successful yet lost in life—until her right-hand man, Poncho, was killed in a car crash with his sister. Two small acts of gratitude at the funeral changed Susana's life forever.

"I was astonished when Poncho's mother prayed over her two dead children," Susana recalled. "She praised God! She prayed that God would use the deaths of her children to impact other lives for His purpose. She thanked Him for His provision!

"Then, the small church putting on the funeral needed more money in order to properly bury Poncho and his sister. He lived in a poor community of seventy-five or a hundred people. The priest stood up and asked the congregation for money."

Wearing plastic shoes and a dirty dress, an elderly woman walked by Susana. "The old plastic purse she clutched was yellow in color from age. I could see it contained several coins. I watched in amazement as this woman emptied her coins into the collection plate."

Two women in hopeless living conditions facing tragic circumstances chose not to dwell on the challenges and uncertainties before them and trusted in the unseen: God's plan.

Their gratitude made an eternal impact on Susana. She was transformed from a leader lost in life to a leader who lives for the lost,
the least, and the left out. Trusting in the unseen and developing the
gift of appreciation will have an eternal influence on you and those
around you.

Discover the Gift of Appreciation

The best way to show my gratitude to God is to accept everything, even my problems, with joy.
—Mother Teresa, who was plagued with poor health, heart problems, pneumonia, and malaria

It is only with gratitude that life becomes rich.
—Dietrich Bonhoeffer, who courageously opposed Nazism and Hitler's anti-Semitic policies and spent years in prisons and concentration camps until he was executed by hanging

I thank God for my handicaps; for through them, I have found myself, my work, and my God.
—Helen Keller, who was deaf, mute, and blind

It has seemed to me fit and proper that [the gifts of God] should be solemnly, reverently, and gratefully acknowledged with one heart and voice by the whole American people. I do therefore invite my fellow citizens . . . to set apart and observe the last Thursday of November next, as a day of Thanksgiving and Praise to our beneficent Father who dwelleth in the Heavens.
—Thanksgiving Proclamation by Abraham Lincoln, who led America through its worst moment in history while beset with depression

Surrounded by poverty, unjustly imprisoned, severely handicapped, and facing uncertainty and adversity, yet living joy-filled lives of gratitude. What's so different about these four individuals? I believe it's perspective.

On a warm summer evening not long ago, my six-year-old daughter, Grace, and I gazed up at the night sky. Shocked, Grace declared, "There aren't any stars in the sky!" Because she couldn't see them behind the cloudy haze, she assumed they were gone.

We're encouraged to make decisions based on solid evidence.

Like Grace, our response is often based on what we believe is true, what is tangible, and what is seen. Unfortunately, we can miss God's plan, His gifts, and His guidance.

Appreciation includes two components: discernment and gratitude. It's the ability to discern the hidden value of something (or someone) and to express gratitude for that particular value or quality. Appreciation is intimate, personal, and unique to an individual.

An art dealer, for example, may observe details in a work of art and be in awe of its uniqueness and beauty. A wine connoisseur may detect the subtle qualities of a fine wine and fully savor the experience. A new mother may take in every nuance of her newborn and revel in his warmth. We each perceive and treasure different aspects of God's gifts; we see Him at work where others either can't or choose not to. Appreciation, then, is discerning or discovering through our perspective and then expressing gratitude for our discovery.

It takes a discerning eye to see God at work in the midst of today's fast-paced world of deadlines, distractions, and distortions. It takes a discerning heart to notice the beautiful in the plain, the appealing in the appalling, and the significant in the insignificant, mundane, and little things in life. Therefore, acquiring the art of appreciation requires both the hard work of an apprentice learning a craft and the natural expression of an artist at work.

Mother Teresa, Dietrich Bonhoeffer, Helen Keller, and Abraham Lincoln understood the value of God *in their work* and expressed their appreciation *through their work*. Through appreciation, their work became a form of worship in the everyday trenches of life.

For these mountain movers, appreciation was manifested in lifelong works of abundance and significance that would inspire generations to come. These lives filled with joy, abundance, and gratitude changed the world through their perspective. Ultimately, they didn't consider themselves great saints, ministers, educators, or presidents but rather apprentices serving a great God. They expressed gratitude through their work as they diligently served a greater purpose beyond themselves. In short, they journeyed from gray to great.

The Five Results of Appreciation

Appreciation does five things. It transforms our grayness into greatness, helps us focus on what we have rather than what we don't have, increases our worth as leaders and establishes a legacy, improves our personal health and well-being, and creates successful workplaces and improves profitability. Let's take a closer look at the five benefits of appreciation.

1. Appreciation Transforms Grayness into Greatness

The journey from gray to great isn't reserved just for celebrated leaders, but for all who accept the gift of appreciation. We transform our grayness into greatness through grace and gratitude.

Grace in the gray. We experience grace in the gray when we discern God's grace at work in the midst of difficult and uncertain circumstances.

Gratitude in the gray. Gratitude in the gray is making a choice to trust in and appreciate God's unseen plan and provision; it's the expression of thanks to God regardless of circumstance.

Grayness to greatness. When we discern God in our work and express gratitude through our work, we become instruments of God's grace. Our expression of gratitude through our work and service to others influences lives.

2. Appreciation Helps Us Focus on What We Have Rather than What We Don't Have

Appreciation is a lost art. The success of this country's economy is based primarily on focusing us on what we *don't* have rather than what we *do* have. Open houses encourage us to think about how our life would be different if we upgraded to a home with an additional room or two. Dealers distract us from the late news with cars that are faster, sexier, and more luxurious than the ones in our garage. Neighbors begin to remodel their kitchens and bathrooms. Our overflowing closets are forced to accommodate another sweater, designer shirt, or pair of shoes. This philosophy that drives the economy carries over to our spiritual life: We focus on what we *don't* have.

The process of moving from gray to great changes our perspective on our circumstances. When we choose to believe that all things are a gift from God, then our families, businesses, and circumstances become gifts to be appreciated, cherished, and valued. When we focus on what we have rather than on what we don't have, we begin to recognize the value of perspective and the gift of appreciation. This provides clarity, even in gray and uncertain times. Someone who understood that appreciation is a gift wrote the following:

> If you woke up this morning with more health than illness, you're more blessed than the million people who will not survive the week.
>
> If you've never experienced the danger of battle, the loneliness of imprisonment, the agony of torture or death or the pangs of starvation, you're ahead of 500 million people in the world.
>
> If you can attend a church meeting without fear of harassment, arrest, torture or death, you're more blessed than three billion people in the world.
>
> If you have food in the refrigerator, clothes on your back, a roof overhead and a place to sleep, you're richer than 75% of the world.
>
> If you have money in the bank, money in your wallet and spare change in a dish someplace, you're among the top 8% of the world's wealthy.
>
> If you're reading this book, you're more blessed than two billion people who cannot read at all.
>
> —Anonymous

Uncertainty and difficulty are often accompanied by impatience and inner turmoil. Choosing to trust in God's unseen plan and dwell on what He's already given brings peace and joy.

3. Appreciation Increases Our Worth as Leaders and Establishes Legacies

Discerning God's guidance and expressing gratitude isn't either a "feel good" pleasantry or a "glass half full" platitude. Appreciation is a core leadership principle whose practical application impacts every facet of life. It's the ability to see God at work and express your sincere thanks in all circumstances. It increases your value as a leader and produces a legacy.

Take Bruce and Dayle Schnack, for example. Their photography studio is small but successful and provides for a decent living. The ups and downs of their family business are similar to those experienced by millions of other small entrepreneurial businesses.

The call that day, from Children's Hospital in Minneapolis, was unusual and urgent: We have a young child who is dying and we need a photographer who can capture these precious family memories before she passes away.

"We're very appreciative of the business we have," Dayle reflected. "We've also been privileged to see our children grow up. We wanted to give thanks to God for His gifts." As a result of that phone call, the Schnacks began a program to help families capture memories of the living and provide portraits to families of terminally ill children—all at no charge to them.

Dayle explains, "It's filled a void in our lives. This has been a labor of love. While this work seems sad, it's not sad to us. We actually receive joy in giving this service to these families—it makes us feel good.

"The service we provide is just a small part of a much bigger picture," she continues. "This work has opened our eyes to another world. These children supply such a blessing in their short lives. We see families coming together in love."

Perspective, appreciation, and gratitude. The Schnacks' legacy is far greater than a portrait on a wall; over two hundred families now have another way to cherish the memories of their beloved children, many who have since passed away.

There's more to Susana's story, too, including a fulfilling legacy to the women of faith who forever impacted her.

Winston Churchill once said, "We make a living by what we get; we make a life by what we give." Susana Espinosa de Sygulla, the young woman whose life was changed by the acts of gratitude displayed at Poncho's funeral, was making a great living, but her life was void. By age twenty-six, Susana had used her gifts in marketing and administration to buy a failing business in Mexico and transform it into a successful venture. She was also working for Dupont, where she trained paint salesmen and managers. "I had so much money I got lost," she explains.

Professionally, her business continued to prosper. Personally, Susana lived lavishly but continued to drift with no sense of purpose. The one bright spot in her life was Poncho, her driver and personal assistant. While only nineteen years old, Poncho brought a sense of stability into her life. "Poncho had a strong faith. He was always respectful of me yet also had the courage to challenge me. He would say, 'God has given you many gifts, but you're wasting them.'

"One day Poncho came to me to ask permission to go to California in search of work. Even though he worked for me, he needed more money to support his family, so I reluctantly supported his trip to the United States.

"I came to work on a Monday morning not long after and was told that Poncho's mother had come to the office to see me. Immediately, I sensed something was wrong. As I drove up the long and dusty dirt road to Poncho's house, I was struck by the poverty. The houses were makeshift shacks, made of pieces of wood and automobile parts built into the side of a hill. As I approached his house, I thought, *These people have nothing and I spend all my money on partying.* I remembered Poncho's words to me and thought, *I'm wasting my life! What am I doing?* When I got to his house, I was amazed that the house was just one room—a kitchen and beds.

"It was there I learned that Poncho and his sister had been killed in a car crash. Poncho's mother had one request for me. 'Please bring my kids home,' she pleaded." Susana agreed and arranged for Poncho and his sister to be brought back to Guadalajara for the funeral. Her heart, however, wasn't in the right place. "I felt tremendous anger toward God. I kept asking God, 'Why do these people live so poor? Why did you allow the one source of income for this family to be killed?'"

Then came the funeral and the faithful actions of two women—Poncho's mother thanking God and asking Him to use the deaths of her children to impact others, and the elderly woman dumping her coins into the collection plate.

"I remember crying to myself, 'What's in her heart where she can give everything and I reluctantly give one peso?' I prayed, 'Lord, help me to value what it means to give. I want to use my gifts and abilities to serve your people.' It was then the Lord transformed my heart."

Poncho's mother and the elderly woman trusted in the unseen—God's plan and provision—rather than living only in the plight and tragedy that surrounded them. They had no way of knowing that their faith and gratitude would eventually impact thousands of people.

Susana sold her business and gave the proceeds to Poncho's family. Today, she's the leader of a non-profit service agency called Go-Latino! in the heart of Minneapolis's Hispanic community. She uses her gifts generously to serve others. She began her career making a living by getting; today she is making a life by what she gives. The evidence lies in the people who see her every day.

"She had 350 kids in our computer learning lab, 1,500 men play-ing soccer, and 25,000 people coming to Mexican Independence Day," said Art Erickson, Urban Ventures founder and CEO. "She works at the highest level of leadership and does it for the least, the last, the lost and the left out."[1]

Juan Morales, 25, a player in Susana's Azteca Soccer League, ex-plained, "Her goal isn't just mentoring soccer. It's changing lives. I was a nothing. And now I'm somebody. If it wasn't for her, I wouldn't be the leader that I am."[2]

And thus goes the process from gray to great. One woman emp-ties her purse in gratitude to God and fills the heart of another. One woman praises God in death and new life is given to another. Two women of humble means with little to be thankful for express appreciation to God and they impact a life. The one whose life is made new goes on to impact thousands of lives, one at a time. Juan Morales is just one of those people. Who will Juan Morales become? Maybe he'll be the first Hispanic president of the United States. Maybe he'll be a great dad. What about the other thousand people? Who will each of them become? The legacy of two humble women of faith now numbers thousands of people whose lives have been impacted for good.

In a world of uncertainty, one thing is certain: One small gesture of gratitude can transform grayness to greatness and leave a legacy for generations to come.

4. Appreciation Improves Our Personal Health and Well-being

Gratitude and appreciation have another personal and professional benefit—they improve our health and well-being. Robert A. Emmons of the University of California, Davis, is one of the foremost author-ities on gratitude. Here are some highlights and findings from his Research Project on Gratitude and Thankfulness, co-investigated by Michael E. McCullough of the University of Miami:[3]

❖ *Physical health* Those who kept gratitude journals on a weekly basis exercised more regularly, reported fewer physical symptoms, felt better about their lives as a whole and were more optimistic about the upcoming week compared to those who recorded hassles or neutral life events. (Emmons and McCullough, 2003)

❖ *Personal goal attainment* Participants who kept gratitude lists were more likely to have made progress toward important personal goals (these included academic, interpersonal, and health-based goals).

❖ *Energy level* In a sample of adults with neuromuscular disease, a 21-day gratitude intervention resulted in greater amounts of high energy, positive moods, a greater sense of feeling connected to others, more optimistic ratings of one's life, and better sleep duration and sleep quality.

❖ *Well-being* Grateful people report higher levels of positive emotions, life satisfaction, vitality, and optimism, and lower levels of depression and stress.

In an interview with *WebMD Health* titled "Boost Your Health with a Big Dose of Gratitude," Dr. Emmons was asked, "How is it that people manage to feel grateful in the face of challenging life circumstances while others sink in despair?" He responded, "So much of gratitude is about one's perspective and framework for looking at the world and at [one]self. People who tend to be mindful of the benefits they received tend to focus their attention outward."[4]

Dr. Emmons reinforces an important point: Appreciation and gratitude don't result from looking at the positive and avoiding the negative. "Grateful people do not deny or ignore the negative aspects of life," his survey results clarify.

Appreciation has everything to do with how we view our lives in relation to God's plan. Is our attention focused inward on ourselves or outward toward others? Do we believe the world revolves around us, or do we see ourselves as part of God's greater plan and purpose? Do we feel entitled to a better life than the one we have or are we grateful for all we've been given? The answer lies in our perspective.

5. Appreciation Creates Successful Workplaces and Improves Profitability

An appreciative leader is more spiritually, mentally, and physically capable of leading others. Not only does appreciation provide personal benefits to one's overall well-being, it provides a healthier outlook to serve in challenging, uncertain times.

Professionally, expressing appreciation plays a part in businesses' success. Disengagement is a significant issue in today's marketplace. A book released by the Gallup Organization, *12: The Elements of Great Managing,* cites the following: "Disengagement-driven turnover costs businesses millions of dollars every year. Replacing an entry-level or frontline employee costs 25% to 80% of that person's annual wage. Replacing an engineer, a nurse, a salesperson, or other specialist costs between 75%–400% of his or her annual salary."[5]

Employees often cite "lack of respect" as the reason for leaving a company. If you were to peel back the onion on "lack of respect," it would be more accurately described as failing to appreciate an employee's value. Leaders who utilize the art of appreciation not only seek out hidden gifts and talents in their employees, they also affirm and express appreciation for employee contributions.

Appreciative leaders play an important role in creating successful workplaces. The same Gallup research on disengaged employees cited the following positive news for leaders who facilitate workplaces that promote engaged employees: "In companies that are better places to work, millions of small actions—statistically insignificant in isolation—created higher customer scores, reduced absenteeism, led to fewer accidents, boosted productivity and increased creativity, accumulating to make a more profitable enterprise."[6]

Appreciation transforms our grayness into greatness, helps us focus on what we have rather than on what we don't have, increases our worth as leaders and establishes legacies, improves our personal health and well-being, and creates successful workplaces and improves profitability. Each of the five results of gratitude is individually important and would alone be a compelling reason to discover the gift of appreciation. Together, they show the immense significance of appreciation on our personal and professional lives.

Mentor on a Mission

Fred Harburg believes that appreciation is a fundamental business leadership trait in adverse and uncertain times. Fred is a leadership expert who's been the internal and external organizational architect for many Fortune 100 companies, including IBM, General Motors, Disney, and AT&T. He's currently the managing partner of Harburg Consulting, LLC.

Fred speaks passionately from his experience that leaders make the difference and that organizations that intelligently cultivate and equip leaders to fully engage themselves and the energy of their people consistently outperform those that do not. As an expert in human motivation in the business arena, Fred was excited to talk about the practical benefits of gratitude and appreciation for business leaders.

Q: What key issues face business leaders today?

A: There have never been more uncertain times. Leaders are inundated with information. They're bombarded with bad news, from a pending bird flu epidemic to global warming to terrorism to stock market fluctuations.

Leaders are uncertain about the future and are preoccupied with their own image. They feel they must look calm and self-assured. In reality, they're like ducks on the water; on the surface they appear calm, but under the surface they're paddling like mad.

Q: How does gratitude contribute to making a leader more effective?

A: In closely observing senior leaders from many walks of life, I've seen that genuine gratitude in the face of adversity is an attitude—perhaps *the* attitude—that most distinguishes the great from the good. The key is perspective. What happens when the chips are down, things look bleak, and you're under intense pressure to produce? A person who maintains gratitude in the midst of uncertainty and adversity maintains a greater perspective beyond his self-interest.

Q: What impact does expressing gratitude or showing appreciation to others have on an organization's success?

A: It has an enormous return benefit. Expressing gratitude and showing appreciation to employees in difficult times is counterintuitive in business. But when leaders express gratitude to employees, employees and customers intuitively recognize and respond to it.

Why is it so important? First, gratitude is the key to an authentic emotional connection. Second, it's the basis for emotional resilience. Finally, it unlocks the potential for the employee to go above and beyond what's required. When the public experiences the results of gratitude, it has a significant positive impact on the organization's reputation and relationship with others.

Q: What practical advice would you give readers of God Is My Coach*?*

A: There are two prevailing theories regarding behavior. People behave their way to new forms of thinking, and people think their ways to new behaviors. My research is yes, both are true. They reinforce each other. Small acts of gratitude will help cultivate a mind-set of gratitude. And a mind-set of gratitude manifests itself in acts of gratitude.

Regardless of your approach, continually be on the lookout for opportunities to appreciate others. We're surrounded with those opportunities; from teachers to neighbors to law enforcement officers and beyond. It's a noble pursuit. It's good for you and good for them.

Counsel for Consideration

*Gratitude unlocks the fullness of life. It turns what we have into enough,
and more. It turns denial into acceptance, chaos into order, confusion into
clarity. . . . It turns problems into gifts, failures into success, the unexpected
into perfect timing, and mistakes into important events. Gratitude makes
sense of our past, brings peace for today and creates a vision for tomorrow.*

—Melody Beattie

One of the most frequently asked questions I receive is, Am I
in God's will? We want to know we're in God's will and doing the
right thing but find our circumstances chaotic and confusing. God
clarifies part of His will for us in 1 Thessalonians 5:16–18: *Be joyful
always; pray continually; give thanks in all circumstances, for this is God's
will for you in Christ Jesus.*

I've been through many periods of uncertainty and adversity. In one
of them, I had been fired from my job, was on the brink of financial
disaster, and was dealing with debilitating back pain. I questioned God's
command to be thankful. You want me to be joyful in the midst of
fear and pain? You want me to give thanks for these circumstances? I
asked. 1 Thessalonians 5:16 was unreachable, or so I thought. The lens
through which I read these verses was clouded by a nearsighted view of
my problems, compounded by impatience and a sense of entitlement.

Now I understand. These verses aren't unrealistic burdens;
they're liberating life principles. They're God's practical prescription
for a successful and significant life.

1. ***Be joyful always*** Joy is a deep understanding that God dwells
in every aspect of your life, regardless of your circumstances. Joy requires trusting in the unseen promises of God rather than in tangible
circumstances.

2. ***Pray continually*** Jesus taught his disciples to persist in pursu-
ing God's guidance. He said, *Ask and it will be given to you; seek and*

you will find; knock and the door will be opened to you (Matthew 7:7). Do you remember what Susana did when she was angry at God? She continued to pray; she kept asking the tough questions.

3. Give thanks in all circumstances Giving thanks is expressing gratitude that God is with us in *all* circumstances. It's God's prescription for maintaining emotional, physical, and spiritual health. Your expressions of thanks benefit you and overflow to others in need of grace. In praising God during her children's funeral, Poncho's mother was given hope and Susana was changed.

It's so easy to get caught up in the day-to-day busyness of life and fail to see and appreciate God's gifts. As much as I love my children, for example, I can easily take the gift of them for granted. When I'm tired from a full day, my bleary eyes often see two kids running through a house overflowing with toys rather than two precious gifts of God who will soon be in bed for the night. One day, I decided to express the gift of appreciation to my daughter, Grace, who was then six. The letter read:

Dear Grace,

I am very proud of you. You love God. You love others. You are smart and do well at school. You are good to Scott and you are a good sister.

You have become a beautiful girl on the outside and on the inside.

I love you very, very much.

Love, Dad

Grace was delighted, but she wondered why I didn't write a letter to Scott. I explained that since he was only two and couldn't read, I didn't think he would really enjoy receiving one. The next morning, I discovered this note:

dear Scotty,

    You ar so preshus.

    I Love You Scotty.

    You ar so Qute.

    You ar the Quttest boy.

    You ar the best.

Love, Grace

Grace proudly presented the letter to him and read it out loud. In reply, Scott ran to Grace and gave her a big hug, exclaiming, "I love you, Grace!"

Appreciation can change a heart. We grieve over the stories of people whose parents pass away without ever sharing a word of praise or encouragement for their children. Other parents have sacrificed much for their children but never received a note of thanks. Good employees have left good jobs simply because they didn't feel appreciated. The smallest word of appreciation can open the door to hope.

Sometimes, we're blessed as God reveals small glimpses of His grace at work that make all our efforts worth it. At other times, we don't see the tangible results of appreciation. Regardless, trust in the unseen and allow the gift of appreciation to govern your perspective.

I must admit that I've struggled with how to articulate the underlying power and significance of appreciation to you. Genuine appreciation gets lost in platitudes. We've all heard them—develop an attitude of gratitude; stop and smell the roses; and the glass is half full versus half empty, among others. These phrases patronize, offend those in difficult circumstances, and keep us from exploring appreciation's true depth and significance. Genuine appreciation in the midst of gray circumstances is choosing to trust in the unseen and focusing on God's plan, provision, and guidance instead of becoming mired in our circumstances.

We may never know the full impact of our choice to be grateful. Maybe choosing to be grateful is just for our own benefit. More likely, it's so God can use our gratefulness to benefit others. Two women of little means experiencing painful circumstances trusted God's plan, His provision, and His guidance. Their words and actions of gratitude resulted in their legacies—Susana's life was changed, resulting in opportunities for thousands. In the same way, if we trust in the unseen, we can trust that our seemingly insignificant gestures of gratitude will result in eternal significance.

4

Platform

The Gift of Your Foundation

Issue: How Do I Live and Communicate My Faith in a Diverse Environment?

Are you familiar with the "Found Out Theory"? It's the fear that one's true self (particularly one's faith) will be found out. The vulnerability comes from the risk of harm from adversarial attack—from being labeled to being libeled, from losing one's reputation to losing one's finances.

I first understood the "Found Out Theory" walking home from school at seven years old, when a teenager stopped me and asked, "Hey kid, are you Jewish?" When I responded in the affirmative, he spit in my face.

Years later, as a follower of Jesus Christ, I kept my faith a private matter. One day, I was confronted. A large consulting project included working with the mayor of a growing midwestern city. During a meeting, he began to rant about the people moving into his community. I was shocked as he stereotyped and berated a growing community of Christians. Suddenly, he stopped, turned to me, looked me straight in the eye, and asked, "You're not one of those $#&!* born again Christians, are you?"

My mind quickly calculated the cost and considered my possible responses. I knew he was out of line, but being the mayor, he was in a position of power; he could jeopardize my role in the project. I asked myself, Should I risk being vulnerable and declare where I stand? Or should I play it safe and keep my faith to myself?

Solution: Let Who You Are Speak for What You Believe

Let your light shine before men, that they may see your good deeds and praise your Father in heaven.

—Matthew 5:16

Walking out of the Georgia World Congress Center, I just wanted to go home. It was time to throw in the towel of being self-employed and get a real job. Since I had already rented a car, however, I figured I was committed to keeping my next appointment. As I unlocked the car door I thought the storm clouds gathering overhead were an interesting metaphor for how I felt inside.

By the time I reached Bill Hardman's office, I was a wreck. Already ten minutes late, I made a run for the front door—soaked, exasperated, and totally defeated. Let's just say I wasn't wearing my best "sales hat" when I met Bill.

Jumping up from his desk chair, Bill greeted me with a smile and a warm handshake. He offered me a cup of hot coffee while he rearranged the two guest chairs so they would be face-to-face. With a deep southern accent, Bill gushed, "I'm so glad you're here. I've been looking forward to meeting you. I had an opportunity to speak to Greg about you and he spoke very highly of you."

His words were like salve on a wound. *I'm glad you're here. I've been looking forward to meeting you. Greg speaks highly of you.* Within thirty seconds, Bill Hardman had diffused my feelings of defeat and discouragement.

So how does one share one's faith in a diverse environment? Hiding who you are and what you stand for isn't the solution. Neither is imposing who you are on others. What is the solution? *Let who you are speak for what you believe.*

Discover the Gift of Your Foundation

Who you are speaks so loudly I can hardly hear what you are saying.
—Ralph Waldo Emerson

We each have a platform. Our platform is our foundation—the principles and beliefs on which we stand. Our platform clarifies and describes who we are to the world. We communicate who we are every day—through our words and actions.

The diverse viewpoints of society often promote an either/or mentality. The media reports daily on the international, national, and local clashes of ideologies and beliefs. From childhood to business, we're taught to compete and win against the opponent. The result is a "fight or flight" mentality that carries over to our platforms: Fight for your beliefs until you "win" or hide your beliefs so as not to be vulnerable to attack.

We are confronted with three choices. First, we can choose a side and impose our beliefs on another. This choice repels others because it reveals our arrogance. The second choice is to remain silent, to avoid attack from different viewpoints. While it may appear "safe," remaining silent about your beliefs repels others by communicating distance and a lack of caring. Finally, we can try to placate all sides by straddling a middle ground. Playing the middle, however, communicates a lack of conviction. As the saying goes, "If you stand for nothing, you'll fall for anything." Billy Graham tells the Civil War story of the men who wore blue coats and gray pants, closing with, "They were shot from both sides."

Face to face with the mayor who demanded to know whether I was a Christian, I denied rather than declared the principles on which I stand. Not wanting to risk the loss of my reputation or the account, I stuffed the gift God gave me—the gift of my platform— for self-preservation.

Thankfully, there's another choice.

It was June 1993 when I met Bill Hardman. I had gone three months in a row without a single speaking engagement or consulting job. I had sixty days to produce revenue or my business was going to fold. Along with the financial pressure came an increasing level of doubt in God's promise for provision as well as in my own confidence and self-worth. I kept asking, Lord, is this really the career you called me to or is it time to quit?

Gray and uncertain times seem to produce even more grayness and uncertainty. I had received an opportunity to attend the Meeting Planners International Conference in Atlanta and participate in a "Speakers Showcase." I would present a twenty-minute speech in front of meeting planners who would potentially buy my speaking services for future conventions. The catch was that I would have to pay my own way. I was torn.

Then I remembered previously chatting with a prospect, Bill Hardman, about facilitating a strategic planning session for his Atlanta-based board of directors. *Why not go see this guy?* I thought. *If he agrees to see me, I'll go. If not, I won't.* With my fallback appointment secure, I decided to go to Atlanta.

Finally, the big day arrived. I dreamed about giving my inspirational speech and receiving a standing ovation from 500 meeting planners. I just knew I would receive invitations to speak all over the world.

"Devastated" hardly describes my emotions when I saw a mere thirteen meeting planners in the room. Those who did come were there for the food, not my speech. A few were polite; others chomped on fruit-filled danishes and read their programs. Some walked out in the middle. Ironically, the absolute failure of this venture brought total clarity to my indecision: My speaking and consulting career was over.

And then came my meeting with Bill. By the time we began to discuss my services, I felt a renewed sense of purpose. Inhaling Bill's encouragement, I spoke with confidence.

Bill hired me to facilitate his board retreat and his staff retreat. The bookings breathed life into a business and a person gasping for air. Over the ensuing months and years, Bill became my greatest salesperson. Thanks to his efforts, I was booked in every state in the Southeast.

Seven years later, I was putting the final touches on *God Is My CEO* and Bill Hardman came to mind. I realized that my business had flourished from the moment I met him. I decided to call and thank him for being there at my moment of greatest need. In his native southern accent, Bill exclaimed in astonishment, "I had no idea! Well, I'm honored to have been of help."

Bill didn't wake up that stormy day and think, *I'm going to make a difference in someone's life today!* Neither did he say, *How am I going to share my faith today?* Very simply, Bill woke up being Bill. He let who he was speak for what he believed. His actions and words spoke for him. Bill Hardman is a regular guy who reflects the love and compassion of Jesus by respecting and caring for those he comes into contact with, whether they be a staff person, a board member, or a visiting consultant from Minneapolis.

Over the last fifteen years, I've conducted hundreds of staff and board retreats and strategic planning sessions. The primary goal is typically to encourage mutual respect, open communication, and team unity as a basis for moving the strategic plan forward. These ideals, however, are the exception rather than the rule. Instead, most sessions are fraught with a lack of respect, hidden agendas, and adversarial turf wars.

I've also had the opportunity to conduct several of Bill's staff and board retreats. While they've been spirited with diverse viewpoints, ultimately they've been based on the love and respect that enable diverse stakeholders to join together in unity and common purpose.

Do you know what the small plaque on Bill's desk reads? *Let your light shine before men, that they may see your good deeds and praise your Father in Heaven.* That's what Bill does.

The Four Principles for Effective Platform

To help us find direction regarding how to communicate our faith effectively in a diverse and pluralistic world, we'll look at the life of Jesus of Nazareth. Jesus used His platform to communicate His principles and beliefs. Communication has four dimensions: actions and words, both public and private. Therefore, we'll look at *what* and *how* Jesus communicated—how He used His platform, privately and publicly, in both words and actions, and then discover how we can apply some of these principles to make our own platform clearer and more effective.

Reflect

Reflection has two meanings. First is to think quietly and calmly; it's an inward look at ourselves as we form an opinion or thought. The second is an outward expression of our thoughts and opinions, a result of our inward reflection. Both our inward reflection and our outward expression display our true image.

The Sermon on the Mount (Matthew 5–7) was Jesus' first recorded public appearance. He wanted people to reflect on what He said, and He wanted people to communicate their newfound beliefs by reflecting who they are as living examples.

The first part of His speech was provocative—He was as radical and explosive as a radio shock jock. Rather than inciting the worst in people, though, Jesus encouraged the best, describing how a person can be blessed. What was radical was *how* He described those who are blessed. Rather than imposing a series of demands, commands, and "how-tos," He contrasted God's view of successful living with the world's view. (*Blessed are those who mourn*, for example, *for they will be comforted* and *Blessed are the meek, for they will inherit the earth.*) Rather than ask people to capitulate to His way of thinking, He challenged them to think for themselves. He didn't look down on people. He challenged them to look inward and, in freedom, form their own opinions and determine their own direction.

Jesus then taught them how to communicate their new beliefs and principles to others. *"Let your light shine before men, that they may see your good deeds and praise your Father in heaven."* In essence, Jesus says: If you believe in me and my teachings, values, and principles, then live them. Let who you are speak for what you believe. Be a role model and practice what you preach. Let your outward actions, decisions, behaviors, and communication reflect your inner beliefs and attitude. Let your nature and character be a living example of your faith.

Jesus used the principle of reflection throughout his ministry. As a teacher, He knew that the best way to impart a principle to others is to show them through example rather than telling them what to do. Think about how Jesus taught the disciples the meaning of serving others: Jesus Christ, the King of kings and Lord of lords, washed the feet of his disciples.

One of my favorite stories in *God Is My CEO* is the story of Jake, the shoeshine guy. I had just left a meeting of surgeons and was angry—angry that they cared more about themselves than their patients. I hopped up on the shoeshine stand, fuming about the self-serving arrogance of these wealthy physicians. Within a few minutes, I found myself relaxing as Jake washed off my muddy shoes. He then meticulously polished my shoes. All the while, Jake shared his appreciation of God's gifts, demonstrated excellence in his craft and through his actions, reflected his love of serving others. Over the past seven years, I've used Jake's story as an example of servant leadership. Just two years ago, however, I realized that Jake was really "washing my feet"!

I've learned more about servant leadership from small gestures like these than from any leadership course. As I studied the brief life of Jesus, I discovered that His ministry consisted less of grand public speeches and more of small and intimate encounters with people like you and me.

We are a reflection of what we think and do in every moment. The smallest of gestures, whether serving a cup of coffee or shining a shoe, can significantly impact another. A wonderful blend of thoughtful intention and natural spontaneity comes with reflection. Perhaps the best way to communicate our faith is to consider our life as one brief but significant teachable moment consisting of a series of small and seemingly insignificant moments. They may come at the most unlikely time and in the most unlikely of circumstances. Sometimes people don't need to be told anything; they simply need to see the light in you to point them in the right direction.

Respect

God places high value on the dignity and worth of all people—rich and poor, friend and foe. Clearly, our actions toward all should be based on love and respect. But what does God say about our words?

> *For out of the overflow of the heart the mouth speaks. The good man brings good things out of the good stored up in him, and the evil man brings evil things out of the evil stored up in him. But I tell you that men will have to give account on the day of judgment for every careless word they have spoken.*
> —Matthew 12:34–36

While the "golden rule" (Do unto others as you would have them do unto you) is known by most cultures and religions, granting respect and dignity to others has become far less prevalent. Language is used as a weapon to gain competitive advantage. The playground nursery-rhyme chant "Sticks and stones will break my bones but words will never hurt me" is wrong; words are powerful and they inflict harm.

Though a lack of respect has permeated our culture, I believe that the vast majority of people are good people who desire to respect others. However, the pressures placed upon us are so great that we can inadvertently disrespect others through our words and actions. A political candidate who is slandered by an opponent drags his opponent's name through the mud in order to compete. A business leader who is challenged by financial pressure and deadlines doesn't fully listen to and engage employees, creating an environment where they feel used and disrespected. In today's highly competitive and pressurized world, respecting others, while a noble concept, often takes a backseat to survival and personal gain.

Showing respect is a powerful communication tool. On the deepest level, people want to be respected and affirmed as people of value and worth. Leaders who connect with others at this level will become significant.

Bill Hardman provided me with something I desperately needed: respect. He did some basic things. He greeted me as a welcomed guest. He expressed interest in me as a person. He listened to me. He accepted me as an equal. He recognized and valued my talents. He encouraged me. Each was a small act demonstrating respect, but together they became a turning point in my career.

You communicate who you are to the world in every aspect of your life—your actions, your decisions, and your words. Your platform, then, is a function of who you are (your heart) and what flows from your heart (words and deeds).

Remember, you have no idea who might need you to be their "Bill Hardman" today.

Reconcile

If a tree falls in the woods but no one is around to hear it, does it make a sound? Communication today is often like the crashing tree: we may make noise but we don't communicate. A lack of communication remains a commonly cited business issue. Near as I can tell, there's never a shortage of talking but there's a pretty common lack of connection.

Communication is a connection—it takes a transmitter and a receiver. When the information imparted by the transmitter is recon-
ciled or brought into harmony with that understood by the receiver,
a connection is made and communication is established.

In a world of ever-increasing diversity, communication becomes a greater challenge. At issue is the connection. Two trans-
mitters turn up the volume only to find there's no receiver. Like
a forest full of trees crashing down, there's lots of noise but no
communication. Growing diversity coupled with increased noise
equals division. Division leads to destruction. From division
within a family to division within a nation to division among nations, the issue remains the same. Jesus understood the dangers of
division when He warned, *Every kingdom divided against itself will
be ruined, and every city or household divided against itself will not stand*
(Matthew 12:25).

We all understand that communication is a key element of leadership. We can also agree that leadership is about connecting people to a common purpose. When Jesus talks about reconciliation,
though, He makes an important point: you can't communicate your
love of God and stand on His principles if you're in conflict. It's a
hypocrisy that destroys a leader's credibility. I can't tell you the number of times I've conducted employee team-building sessions only to
have employees point out conflicts between senior management as
stumbling blocks.

Reconciliation has two components. On a personal level, a leader
needs to reconcile his or her professional self with his or her spiritual
core. This process will allow leaders to establish trust and credibility with the ones they lead. Second, the leader needs to reconcile
with others. The ability to create harmony and agreement among
people results in admiration from others. Who doesn't want peace
and harmony in his or her life? Generally, people prefer to work
where people come together for a greater good rather than in settings embattled with conflict and division. If, as a leader, you can

genuinely communicate reconciliation to others, you'll have significant influence.

Division destroys and reconciliation builds. Jesus never stated that we couldn't have diverse viewpoints. He said we needed to find a way to connect in the midst of our diversity. Agreement (see Matthew 18:19) implies accord that is attained by discussion and adjustment of differences. Loving and praying for those with different viewpoints is counterintuitive. If, however, we communicate in the spirit of reconciliation, great things can happen. Within a company, for example, departments with differing opinions should allow the organization's core values or greater good to prevail.

As I mentioned, I facilitated strategic planning sessions for Bill Hardman's board and staff. Of all the sessions I've facilitated, the ones involving Bill's leadership were some of the most successful. I felt God's presence. Bill's teams were excited about accomplishing a greater good. It isn't so much that Bill is a great communicator, leader, or negotiator; it's Bill's attractiveness as a leader. First, you know where he's coming from. His core values and beliefs are clear from his actions. His integrity establishes his credibility. Your views may differ from Bill's, but you can trust him. Second, Bill has the ability to help others reconcile diverse viewpoints. As a leader by example, there are times when he stands firm and there are times when he concedes. His example paves the way for open discussion, adjustment of differences, consensus, and, most importantly, ownership of the vision.

Raise

The two young boys were engaged in verbal battle. With their mothers nowhere nearby, the conversation started with a legitimate difference of opinions but quickly deteriorated into an ever-lowering battery of insults and name-calling. "You're an airhead!" shouted the first boy. "You're a double airhead!" replied the other.

I marveled at the wonder of testosterone as I went inside to watch one of my favorite news programs. Two candidates debated a particular issue. The debate began as each individual intelligently articulated his respective viewpoint. Within minutes, the debate deteriorated into insults and name-calling. "Senator, you're a bigot!" "No," replied the senator, "you're the bigot!"

Here's my challenge to you. The next time you turn on the TV, regardless of the nature of the show you're watching, make a simple evaluation. Ask yourself, Does the content of the material as well as the interaction and communication between the characters add or subtract or raise or lower your opinion of the human spirit?

What if you asked the same question of each person who observed or interacted with you in the last week? How would your evaluation form look?

Raise is the culmination of the first three Rs. Reflect, respect, and reconcile all contribute to raising the dignity and value of mankind as a reflection of God. When Jesus came to earth, the two most important things He wanted to talk about were God and people. One of the greatest gifts He gave people was the freedom and right to choose. He never forced His opinions on others, and He respected their right to choose. He respected this right even to the point of crucifixion.

Raise has multiple definitions. It means raising a question instead of demanding an answer. Raising the spirit of another instead of putting another down. Raising the level of communication from conflict to civility. Raising the dignity and worth of another instead of lowering yourself to the insults of another. Raising the standards of excellence instead of accepting the mediocrity of political correctness. Each of these definitions points upward toward a higher level of communication—one that honors God and others.

The Apostle Paul shares his thoughts on raising our communication through words and deeds in Philippians 4:8–9:

Finally, brothers, whatever is true, whatever is noble, whatever is right, whatever is pure, whatever is lovely, whatever is admirable—if anything is excellent or praiseworthy—think about such things. Whatever you have learned or received or heard from me, or seen in me—put it into practice. And the God of peace will be with you.

As leaders, communicators, and teachers, we are to be a reflection of all that is right, excellent, admirable, and uplifting so others can see, hear, observe, and learn. This is the standard with which we honor God and others through our platform.

Mentor on a Mission

In my opinion, Dr. Os Guinness is one of the most insightful people of this generation. His book, *The Call: Finding and Fulfilling the Central Purpose of Your Life*, goes past superficial understanding to the heart of what calling means. Dr. Guinness sat down with me to talk about platform.

Q: What do you see as the main issue facing Christians who want to live and share their faith in today's diverse culture?

A: The real challenge for faith is in the heartland of the modern world because of the way the world has squeezed us into its mold. We're also at a critical stage in American culture. So people of faith today have a tremendous challenge living their faith and being salt and light, as faith is counterintuitive to the norms of our culture. A mark of a culture in decline is to turn against its "old" faith and turn to any weird, wild, and wonderful "new" faith. And of course, in America the Christian faith is the "old faith." As a result, a tremendous amount of baggage comes with the word *Christianity*, and with it prejudice and disdain.

Q: Explain further the baggage that comes with the word Christianity.

A: Put simply, we are associated with the evils and excesses of the centuries of Christendom, such as the Inquisition or the scandals of leaders today with their pants down and their foot in their mouth. But think of it on a more common level. Take the words *Christ, Christian,* and *Christianity.* As you move from the first to the second to the third, you shift from *Christ*, which is simple, fresh, immediate, and personal, to *Christian*, which is more institutional, to *Christianity*, which is more ideological. In other words, the connotations become more impersonal and negative. In addition, scholars and journalists alike want to pin labels on people and that contributes to the reductionism of our modern thinking too.

Q: What do you see as the key issue facing business leaders who live and communicate their faith in such a diverse and public environment?

A: I might mention a hundred issues, but many CEOs tell me their number-one issue is honesty. In our postmodern age, many leaders live in a gray world of euphemisms, half-truths, lies, hype, and spin. Evasion of the truth is epidemic. Yet business depends on trust and trust depends on truth, so truth is a deeply important thing for human beings. Leaders need to demonstrate that faith isn't just a matter of belief but a habit of the heart.

Q: How do you communicate your faith?

A: St. Francis gave the best advice: "Preach the Gospel constantly, and if necessary, use words." So a life lived well is the clearest statement we can make. When it comes to actually sharing our faith, I always try to start by listening to others and their stories. I then go to asking questions. I only share the positive answers of the Gospel when I am sure people are either open and ready or show they are really seekers. In their eagerness to witness, or under the pressure of guilt, many Christians say far too much and far too soon and only leave people as burned-over ground.

Q: What practical advice can you give today's businessperson who wants their faith to make a difference in their world?

A: First, count the cost. As the wider world moves further and further from its Christian roots, we become more and more different and that can be very costly. Second, count on your major impact coming from your life and overall witness, rather than any words. Third, be sure to join a support group of peers outside your work, people who can provide fellowship, inspiration, encouragement, and accountability. None of us dares go it alone today. We are rarely stronger than the band of friends who are our ultimate network as we live before our one audience: The Audience of One.

Counsel for Consideration

When I was having lunch with a respected friend, Cary Humphries, he asked me, "What do you think is one of the most important truths in the Bible?" After I stumbled around with some verses, he said, "I believe it's John 3:16: 'For God so loved the world that he gave his one and only Son, that whoever believes in him shall not perish but have eternal life.'"

He then looked at me and said, "Here is one of the most important truths in the Bible and Jesus communicated this message not publicly to thousands but to one person, Nicodemus, in private at night."

Think about it. On any given Sunday during football season, someone will hold up a sign that says JOHN 3:16, presumably to share his faith. Is that how Jesus meant for His message to be shared? I don't think He did—I believe He intended His message to be shared as a personal dialogue between two people.

Dr. Guinness was right when he said, "Expect prejudice." I felt the prejudice when that teenager spit in my face after I told him I was Jewish. When we share our faith in inappropriate ways, we invite prejudice. The "John 3:16 sign" approach causes believers to be labeled as proselytizers and religious fanatics, both of which builds walls between people of faith and others. Jesus meant for us to share our faith in everyday situations.

There's no set formula for sharing your faith. We each have to find our own unique way. Jesus tells us to be "as wise as serpents and innocent as doves." As leaders, we need to exhibit wisdom, show sensitivity to our environments and be appropriate for the circumstances when we communicate our faith in such challenging and prejudicial environments.

As Jesus said, "For out of the overflow of the heart the mouth speaks." I believe that if you love God with all your heart and you love others, your communication will honor God and connect with the one person who needs to experience His grace. How do you live and communicate your faith in a diverse environment? Simply let who you are speak for what you believe. You can trust that people will see the revealed Christ in you and praise your Father in heaven.

5

Power

The Gift of Pressure

Issue: How Can I Keep Pressure from Getting the Best of Me?

I began my career with Hyatt Hotels alongside two other recent college grads. Frank was an energetic self-starter. Jeff was a well-organized leader who excelled in all his college endeavors. They were as different as night and day, yet equally talented and gifted. They jumped out of the gate quickly in their respective fields—Frank in sales and Jeff in food and beverage. Within three years, they had been promoted to sales director and food and beverage director, respectively.

The pressure grew as they climbed through the ranks to higher-level positions. Under the heat of pressure, though, their individual gifts and talents became their downfall.

The self-reliance and ambition that made Frank successful caused him to keep charging ahead. He became a workaholic, spending his weekends at work, away from his family. This led to bouts of alcoholism, two failed marriages, and a career that could never satisfy his expectations.

Jeff's attention to detail first created standards of excellence, but then led to perfectionism and a nervous breakdown at only twenty-eight years of age. He began to seek simpler jobs with less pressure. Eventually, Jeff settled into a safe and secure job that resulted in boredom and apathy.

Under pressure, one (Frank) abused his gifts while the other (Jeff) neglected his gifts. Thinking about Frank and Jeff made me wonder. Might the issue lie not in the pressure itself, but in how we use our God-given gifts under pressure?

Solution: Transform Your Pressure into Power

We have this treasure in jars of clay to show that this all-surpassing power is from God and not from us. We are hard pressed on every side, but not crushed; perplexed, but not in despair; persecuted, but not abandoned; struck down, but not destroyed.

—2 Corinthians 4:7–9

I thought back to my breaking point. I had just received my seventeenth rejection letter from a publisher, and my wife's and my struggle to have a baby had been met with constant disappointment.

Monty and I were having lunch in his office when I broke down and cried as I told him of my decision to abandon my four-year attempt to publish *God Is My CEO*. Monty picked up his Bible, worn from decades of study. Slowly and deliberately, he turned to 2 Corinthians 4:7–9 and in a soft voice started to read.

Then Monty turned to me and said, "Larry, I think the baby and the book have become your idols. Perhaps God is testing and humbling you to see what's really in your heart." Monty's words convicted me to the core.

I had talent, ambition, and self-discipline, but in the end, my thoughts betrayed me. I wanted to fulfill God's call and serve His purpose, but I gave in under pressure.

Understanding that this all-surpassing power is from God didn't eliminate the pressure, but it changed my focus—rather than trying to control my destiny, I partnered with God to fulfill it. In shedding my self-centered purposes, I could be prepared to serve God's greater purpose. In short, it helped me discover God's power—the gift of pressure.

Discover the Gift of Pressure

Pressure is the single most powerful stimulus for growth and an essential part of life. We grow and reproduce spiritually not in the absence of pressure, but because of it.

God has designed each of us with a unique calling and purpose. It's our job to develop the character needed to fulfill our calling. We possess deep within us an innate ability to explore, overcome, and create under pressure. The compelling call of God, then, coupled with our inherent ability to fulfill our call, creates a powerful force. This constructive pressure enables us to fulfill our God-given potential.

We often consider pressure as negative stress (to be dealt with) rather than positive energy (on which to capitalize). In reality, pressure motivates us toward our goals. It strengthens us to tackle and overcome challenging circumstances in our life. Pressure compels us toward excellence and significance. It empowers us to rise to the occasion and prevail over circumstances that threaten to derail us.

The issue, then, lies not with the amount of pressure we face, but with how we employ our gifts under pressure. The external pressure (circumstances) in our lives is less of an issue than the unique way we respond to it. Our success isn't based on what happens, but on what we do with what happens.

We're blessed with an array of gifts. When we employ them wisely and effectively, we can transform pressure into power. This power not only provides clarity of purpose and a renewed sense of direction, but it gives us the strength to lead others through uncertainty.

We also have the choice to neglect or abuse our gifts. The misuse of gifts has destructive power. It induces self-inflicted wounds and harms others.

Therefore, pressure is a double-edged sword. It can be a catalyst for clarity and direction, or it can cause tremendous doubt and confusion. Pressure can be transformed into power, or it can render one powerless. It all hinges on what a person believes and does. Every thought creates a habit. Every habit manifests itself in a behavior and every behavior has a consequence. As James Allen wrote, "As a man thinketh, so he is." It all comes down to how we view (think about) and use (through behaviors, decisions, and actions) our gifts.

The Highway of Life

The illustration on page 87 shows what happens when internal issues or external circumstances (i.e., pressure) begin to complicate our life.

Throughout life, we find ourselves on the center of the road (our power zone), on a shoulder on either side of the road (the subtle shoulders), or on the extreme edge of a shoulder—the ditch.

The power zone represents the ideal state—your sweet spot where you're transforming pressure into power. Your heart, mind, and spirit are working together to fulfill your God-given potential and purpose. You have heightened *awareness* of your environment, you're *aligned* with your purpose, and you're *adapting* under pressure and boldly taking *action,* fully engaged with energy.

Unfortunately, we rarely experience perfect conditions on the highway of life. A regular flow of rainy, foggy, and stormy days slows or derails us from our path to success and significance. We also know we have no control of external conditions; we have only our God-given gifts with which to respond along the way.

The subtle shoulders are transition zones where we risk running off the road. In these zones, our habits or tendencies under pressure take us off course. We often respond to life's pressures in hidden or subconscious ways where we don't even realize how we're thinking or behaving.

There are two distinct shoulders, both of which lead away from constructive pressure and toward negative stress. On one shoulder, we abuse our gifts and on the other, we neglect our gifts.

Bob, for example, tends toward perfectionism and abusing his gifts. When he stays within the boundaries of his power zone, his gifts

The Highway of Life

The Ditch	The Subtle Shoulders (Transition Zone)	Our Power Zone	The Subtle Shoulders	The Ditch
Habits or tendencies under pressure: Neglect our gifts		Full use of gifts	Habits or tendencies under pressure: Abuse our gifts	
Negative stress (increases as we move toward the left)		Positive stress	Negative stress (increases as we move toward the right)	
Examples of Neglecting Gifts Apathy Disengagement Lack of inertia and feeling stuck		*Transforming Pressure into Power* Aware of internal and external pressures Aligned with our purpose Adapting under pressure Taking action and fully engaged	*Examples of Abusing Gifts* Workaholism Adrenaline junkies Abuse of power	
Result? Apathy; derailed from our call and potential		Result? Transform pressure into power; fulfill our call and potential	Result? Burnout; derailed from our call and potential	

include self-discipline, attention to detail, drive, and energy, each of which drives him toward great achievement. Under pressure, however, Bob's "all or nothing" thinking causes reduced productivity as he loses time and energy on small and irrelevant details. He has a strong desire to do things right, but under pressure he procrastinates. Determined to overcome all obstacles to success, he's easily discouraged and depressed by failure. His gifts become his downfall.

Adrenaline junkies use the business world to legitimize abusing their gifts. They get high on achievement. While they express their gifts at work, workaholics can't seem to find satisfaction in relationships at work or at home. Sid Kirchheimer, in a WebMD article titled "Workaholism: The 'Respectable' Addiction," describes a Japanese term, *karoshi*, or death by overwork. It's estimated to cause one thousand deaths per year, nearly 5 percent of that country's stroke and heart attack deaths in employees under age sixty.[1]

Mary, on the other hand, thrives on safety and security and is inclined to neglect her gifts. She's an excellent worker; loyal, conscientious, and thorough. She's customer focused, loves to serve people and see them satisfied, and she thrives under pressure. At least this was true with her previous boss and company. When her company was bought out, the culture changed. A new, unethical leader caused Mary much grief as she began to compromise her values little by little. She wanted to find a new job, but her desire for safety and security created a lack of initiative. She hated her job but felt she couldn't leave. At forty-seven, Mary felt stuck. In her mind, she rationalized that she would look for a new job once her daughter was in college. Disengaging, she did just enough to get by. The lack of pressure to fulfill her potential caused her to neglect her gifts. Over time, atrophy (of her God-given gifts) and apathy made life dull and boring.

Disengaged workers cost U.S. companies billions of dollars each year. A 2001 Gallup study stated that "actively disengaged" employees—those fundamentally disconnected from their jobs— cost the U.S. economy between $292 and $355 billion per year.[2]

The ditches on our "highway" table represent the potential negative consequences of allowing our erroneous thoughts to succumb to pressure. Conventional wisdom tells us to avoid our weaknesses and focus on our strengths. As a result, we unknowingly allow our weaknesses to sabotage our true calling and success.

Where are you on the highway? Are you feeling the power of God's call upon you? Do you tend to abuse your gifts under pressure or neglect them? Do you feel like you're in the ditch? Are you stuck in a rut or have you burned yourself out trying to do too much? Well, here's God's mercy in action. God will meet you at your point of need, wherever that may be. It doesn't matter where you start; what matters is where you go from here.

To move forward, we'll first identify our negative habits and tendencies. Then we'll walk through a four-step process to using God's gifts under pressure.

The Perils of Undetected Bad Habits and Thoughts

We all have habits—some are good and some are bad. A habit is an involuntary behavior that is carried out unconsciously. Even the brightest and most gifted leaders can fall victim to hidden habits and erroneous thoughts. Our blind spots are areas where our thoughts and behaviors can betray us. The very gifts that bring us to the top of the mountain can cause us to stumble back down.

Remember the Olympic snowboarder who lost the gold medal when she fell trying a showboat jump just before the finish line? What about the star pitcher who sat out the remainder of the season after he punched a wall and broke his pitching hand? These gifted athletes let their thoughts get the best of them. Pride took one, and anger got the best of the other.

Business leaders are no different. Erroneous thoughts and bad decisions have had significant consequences for leaders and their respective organizations. Tremendous energy is focused on external factors such as competition and financial pressure when, ultimately, a leader's own thoughts cause him to fail. Fear, greed, lust for power, pride, and selfish ambition are extremely powerful drivers that can lead to decisions with serious and irreparable consequences.

Either/or thinking is pervasive in society today. We live in red states or blue states. We're conservatives or liberals. If our performance falls short of our goals, we've failed. This type of thinking carries over to our faith and results in a double-minded mentality, another form of erroneous thinking. Your beliefs and actions show your faith. One who's double minded wavers back and forth, one day loving God and the next rejecting Him; one day displaying faith and another day indicating a lack of it.

I had been the epitome of a double-minded thinker when Monty's words convicted me to the core. "Larry, I think the baby and the book have become your idols. Perhaps God is testing and humbling you to see what's really in your heart." He was right. Starting a family and writing a book about integrating work and faith were both noble pursuits, but my eyes had become set on the outcome, not the process.

Because we had no baby and I had no contract, I felt that all those years had proven I was a failure. I was focused on what I didn't have instead of what I had. I focused on what would happen to me rather than on what God was doing in me. I wavered between serving my purpose and serving God's purpose. I left Monty's office knowing that if this really was a call of God, then I had to move forward and trust the process, including the pressure that came with it.

Coming to terms with the idea that "the all-surpassing power was from God and not from me" helped me develop a new relationship with God. Rather than trying to control my destiny, I partnered with God to fulfill it. This helped me shed my self-centered purposes and prepared me to serve God's greater purpose. God prepared us not to achieve our goals but to fulfill our roles. It wasn't about achieving a baby—it was about being prepared to serve as a parent. It wasn't about writing a best-seller—it was about helping the one reader who needed to integrate his or her work and faith. It was only then that my heart and my mind were prepared for God's wisdom.

David's Choice

David, the gentle shepherd boy, the courageous slayer of Goliath, the ancestor of Jesus, the beloved and respected leader, and the one God affectionately called "a man after my own heart."

Do you remember David's other names: adulterer? murderer? liar? betrayer?

Few others have engendered more respect for their courage and character than King David. How is that possible when we think of how he abused his God-given authority? I believe that in David's choice is a leadership lesson that applies to each of us today.

In 2 Samuel 7, God promised David, *Now I will make your name great, like the names of the greatest men on earth* and *Your house and Your kingdom will endure forever.* With God's promises came tremendous pressure, but God also provided David with the power to honor and fulfill his calling. David used his God-given gifts to transform Israel into a great military power. But David also had an adulterous affair with Bathsheba and arranged the murder of her husband.

At the height of his rule, David was visited by his trusted counselor, Nathan. Nathan told the story of a rich man, one with a large number of sheep and cattle, who took the sole possession of a poor man—his lamb. David was deeply angered. He replied, *As surely as the Lord lives, the man who did this deserves to die!* Then Nathan said to David, *You are the man!*

As followers of Christ who are as fallible as David, we wonder why God would bestow power upon such a man. Let's consider David's response.

David said to Nathan, *I have sinned against the Lord.*

David confronted the truth head-on. Recognizing his sinful actions and bad thinking, he immediately sought forgiveness and proceeded to get back on the path God had prepared for him. Rather than running from or caving into the pressure, he confronted both the internal blind spots that impeded his calling and the external circumstances of his situation.

In David's choice lies a powerful lesson. God doesn't seek perfect leaders who will be flawless; He seeks flawed leaders who will fulfill His perfect plan. The power to fulfill God's call doesn't come from a lack of pressure but from the transformation of pressure into power.

Pressure and power are inexorably linked: Pressure is the force upon
you to act and power is the force within you that causes you to act.
Godly leaders have the power to fulfill God's call because of their response to the flaws and circumstances that pressure them every day.

Four Steps for Transforming Pressure into Power

David's powerful and honest leadership is revealed through many
of his Psalms. David wrote on four common themes: awareness,
alignment, adaptability, and action. Following this process will place
you in a position to discern and utilize God's gifts under pressure.

Step #1: Awareness—See Your World from God's Perspective

Awareness is an intense, heightened state of alertness regarding
your circumstances. The awareness stage not only helps us discern
any external threats to our well-being, it also helps us discover our
internal blind spots.

Why do we allow ourselves to be blindsided by an outside influence or allow our own thinking to sabotage our success? There's a
two-fold explanation. First, the uncertainty of our circumstances
clouds our judgment. Second, our judgment is flawed. We're all prej-
udiced to some degree—we have preconceived opinions regarding
issues, people, and our circumstances. We often make these judg-
ments with insufficient facts or knowledge. For example, we may
evaluate a person by appearance without knowing his or her character. We may allow our ego to determine which car we buy without
factoring in the full cost of our decision. Maybe we vote political
candidates strictly by party line. In this fast-paced world where time
is at a premium, it's easier to make a quick judgment than to search
out the underlying facts or truth of a matter. The bottom line? We're
not perfect; we need help.

What do we need to do? Replace our imperfect judgment with
discernment and wisdom.

Discernment is the ability to understand something that isn't readily seen. Wisdom is seeing the world from God's perspective; it's a gift that helps you know and do the right thing under pressure. As we're told in Proverbs 24:5, *A wise man has great power.* Wisdom acts like a filter, separating deceptive thinking from God's Truth. It helps you discern right from wrong, truth from fiction, sincere motives from hidden agendas, what's helpful from what's harmful, what's valuable from what's worthless, what's energy building from what's energy draining. Together, discernment and wisdom form a powerful tool to increase our awareness of internal and external threats.

Seeking God's wisdom is a lifelong pursuit of God Himself; it's a diligent search to discover His nature, His character, and His presence. Wisdom comes through prayer, Bible study, and others. James offers specific criteria for helping us know God's wisdom: *But the wisdom that comes from heaven is first of all pure; then peace-loving, considerate, submissive, full of mercy and good fruit, impartial and sincere* (James 3:17). Let's take a closer look at James's criteria.

Pure: Purity is being free of anything that weakens or pollutes your thinking; free of moral fault or guilt. That means you can acknowledge or disclose your worst thoughts and behaviors and God sees you as "not guilty." The clear conscience this produces results in clear thinking.

Peace-loving: Peace is freedom from disturbing, anxious thoughts and emotions. Peace means to bring into harmony. The more you align your thoughts with God's thoughts, the more peace of mind you'll have. Peace of mind produces right thinking.

Considerate: To consider is to think a matter out carefully before forming an opinion. Consideration produces thoughts and decisions that are mindful of the rights and feelings of others.

Submissive: Submission is yielding what's out of your control to God. It means acknowledging that God's wisdom is more effective than your thinking. Humility produces guidance.

Full of Mercy: One who is full of mercy is compassionate toward another even when justice is warranted. Compassion produces a fresh start and new perspective regardless of your past.

Impartial: Impartiality is fair, balanced, right, and just in approach. It gives you the freedom to see and do what is right, free of prejudice, judgment, and emotion.

Sincere: Sincerity is honesty, which allows you to be transparent before God, yourself, and others. Honesty produces clarity.

King David deeply desired that God would reveal his blind spots. In Psalm 139:23 he wrote, *Search me, O God, and know my heart; test me and know my anxious thoughts.* In practical terms, we need to apply the above criteria to our own thoughts and motives. With a clear internal perspective, we can then more clearly consider our external circumstances.

James goes on to explain why we don't receive wisdom and provides a solution for obtaining wisdom. *You do not have, because you do not ask God. When you ask, you do not receive, because you ask with the wrong motives.* His solution? *Come near to God and he will come near to you.*

My daughter, Grace, saw a television commercial advertising an upcoming movie and, with her typical enthusiasm and passion, asked whether she could see it. I explained that the content was inappropriate for her age. While she was initially upset with my response, she began to understand my rationale as we continued to talk about it. Grace's motive for wanting to see the movie wasn't bad, it was uninformed. Acting on her motive would have exposed her to concepts she wasn't ready to handle. In the same way, our thoughts and motives can unintentionally lead us down the wrong path. God is a loving Father who has our best interests at heart. Through awareness, allow His discernment and wisdom to clarify your perspective.

Step #2: Alignment—Transform Negative Tendencies into Creative Tension

God desires that we work *with* Him to accomplish His purposes. The outward expression of our faith is manifested in right thinking, behaviors, and actions. It's not the breadth of knowledge that provides us with clarity and direction, but the depth of our wisdom and the height of our character.

A binocular has two lenses with a dial between them. Without adjustment, the view is blurry. When we adjust the dial and bring the lenses into alignment, we see with greater clarity. The key to spiritual clarity is to bring your view and God's view into a single-minded focus.

Jesus promised us, *In this world you will have trouble* (John 16:33). How, then, can we be aligned with God when we're experiencing negative stress? Through creative tension. Creative tension is healthy and positive pressure as you dialogue with God. We tend to think that an absence of pressure is the healthiest scenario. That's false. The absence of pressure is stagnation; we become apathetic. Pressure is a catalyst that causes us to grow in faith and character.

Tested faith is part of the natural process of growing in character and God's nature. Working through difficulties, doubt, and dilemmas doesn't separate us from God; it unifies us with God. Doubt and difficulty aren't bad. Rather than cause us to descend from our faith, they're a means of growing in faith. Why? When we take steps of faith in the midst of uncertainty, we grow and our faith is strengthened.

There's a difference between creative tension and having a

double-minded mentality. Being double minded is applying an either/or mentality to a dilemma. One visualizes the devil on one shoulder, an angel on the other, and a person's thoughts going back and forth between the two. That's double-minded wavering. Creative tension has an integration mentality—you and the Lord are working toward a common goal. It's the knowledge that progress is born out of pain and difficulty. Engaging in creative-tension dialogue with God allows one to resolve an issue, make a choice, and follow through. Creative tension, then, is a valuable and important part of leading through uncertainty.

Good coaches bring out the best in athletes; they know when to push beyond an athlete's perceived limits and also know when to prescribe rest, healing, or rehabilitation. While the coach and the athlete work together, ultimately, the athlete does the training. That's the kind of relationship God wants with us. Creative tension adds weight to the spiritual muscle-building process.

Another aspect of alignment is role clarification—understanding your role and God's role in the process. God has provided you with gifts, for example, but it's your role to use them wisely. God provides you with wisdom; it's your role to know and do the right thing. God designed you with a purpose; it's your role to develop the character to fulfill your purpose.

Role clarification enhances clarity. You can accomplish this when you:

a. Ask God to give you the wisdom to discern which specific actions are within your control versus actions and things that are out of your control and are God's responsibility.
b. Take charge of the things within your control.
c. Surrender control of the things that are God's responsibility.

God is a loving Father who desires to be one with you. Through alignment, you will become one with God's thoughts and purposes, experience the deepening of your faith through creative tension, and have enhanced ability both to lead and to rest by taking charge of what is within your control and surrendering control of what is God's responsibility.

Step #3: Adaptability—Develop Resiliency in Uncertainty

Adaptability is the ability to modify your thoughts and behaviors to accommodate life's ever-changing circumstances. Adaptability grows by developing resiliency. Resiliency is the process of adapting successfully to difficult or challenging life experiences. It helps us adjust plans when something unexpected arises, bounce back from setbacks, and endure long periods of adversity. The by-products of resiliency are growth, maturity, and fruit-bearing.

Life is filled with adversity and uncertainty, even when you're three years old. Scott's first swimming lesson didn't go well. Blowing bubbles and lying on his back in the water were terrifying to him. He was facing his most significant pressure to date: He had less than twenty-four hours before he had to go back to swim class and face his greatest fear—putting his face in the water. The fresh memories of the day resulted in the "fight or flight" response.

As bedtime drew near, we opted for a team approach. "Let's all go to the bathtub and try to put our faces in the water," we said. Our daughter, Grace, was assigned as head coach and got in the tub with him. Through creative pressure, we challenged Scott to stretch beyond his fear. We cheered, we chanted, and we bribed. It was then that Scott decided that the only person for whom he would be willing to conquer his fear was his twelve-year-old cousin, Kaitlin. With Kaitlin's voice of encouragement on the phone, Scott took a leap of faith and put his face in the water. His joy-filled face emerged dripping from the water to frenzied cheers and high-fives. And then he did it again and again and again.

Love conquered fear not by eliminating it but by prevailing over it. Scott relinquished control because he trusted the ones he loved.

That trust enabled him not to lose control of his life, but to gain control by learning how to adapt.

A little boy, by placing his face in the water, took a step of faith. Just as with Scott, each step of faith we take builds our resiliency. In the words of Charles Reade, "Sow an act and you reap a habit. Sow a habit and you reap a character. Sow a character and you reap a destiny."

Step #4: Action—Wisdom plus Action Equals Obedience

Our personalities are as different and numerous as stars in the sky. Therefore, we respond to pressure in different ways. Some run ahead and act before seeking God's wisdom and timing. Society promotes this, as most business cultures are based on action. Activity equals productivity, sales, and profits. Families can also become overwhelmed with activity and stop growing as a family. This kind of action produces nothing more than busyness. We may believe we have clarity and focus, but we're focused on the wrong thing.

Others diligently seek wisdom but can't seem to act upon it. The Apostle James addressed this in James 1:22: *Do not merely listen to the word, and so deceive yourselves. Do what it says.* Wisdom requires action. Seeking wisdom without action just leads to more confusion. Geoff, for example, was a talented leader looking for a career that matched his gifts and calling. He developed a strategic-planning model for small-business owners that aligned perfectly with his talents, passion, and field of interest, but he was stuck. He got the first part right. He prayed diligently, consulted with trusted peers, and researched the market. But when it came time to act upon what he'd learned, he was unable to follow through. Though he had knowledge, he really didn't have wisdom, because he couldn't follow through on the knowledge he'd gained.

Action without wisdom produces busyness. Thinking without wisdom produces confusion. They're both a waste of precious time and energy.

In the Parable of the Loaned Money, Jesus stated, *You have been faithful with a few things; I will put you in charge of many things*. That's how obedience works—one small act of faith at a time. That's all that's expected of us: to seek God's wisdom and have the faith to act upon it. Obedience is knowing the right thing to do and doing the right thing, one thought at a time, one decision at a time, and one act at a time.

Those are the four steps in the transformation from pressure into power. You now have heightened awareness of your environment, you're fully aligned with your purpose, and you're adapting under pressure and boldly taking action, fully engaged with energy. Your heart, mind, and spirit can now work together to fulfill your God-given potential and purpose.

Mentor on a Mission

Jack Groppel, Ph.D., is vice chairman and co-founder of the Human Performance Institute. He's an internationally recognized authority and pioneer in the science of human performance and an expert in fitness and nutrition. An adjunct professor of management at the J. L. Kellogg School of Management at Northwestern University, Dr. Groppel is also the author of *The Corporate Athlete: How to Achieve Maximal Performance in Business and Life.*

Q: What key issues impede the performance of athletes and business leaders?

A: I believe the key issues that leaders and athletes encounter are "win at all costs" attitudes and fear [of winning or losing].

Q: Describe what it means to face your truth.

A: Facing your truth is to truly own your "stuff." The key word is *own*. At the Human Performance Institute, we've observed that people have five basic ways they lie to themselves: denial, minimizing, blaming, projecting, and numbing out are all ways we deceive ourselves.

Q: What advice would you give to someone who is afraid to confront his or her truth (i.e., a weakness, shortcoming, etc.)?

A: Ask yourself why you're afraid of the truth. Obviously, the truth can hurt, but usually we're afraid of knowing the truth because we perceive that others will judge us or even that we'll judge ourselves.

Q: Describe the concept of oscillation. How does balancing stress and recovery help an individual transform negative pressure into positive power?

A: Oscillation is a basic biological pattern of any living organism. All living creatures are affected by the harmonic action of the seasons, day and night, glucose cycles after eating, sleep cycles throughout the night, EKG from the heart, EEG from the brain, and EMG (electromyography) from the muscles. These each work in cycles of high and low.

However, we typically work and live our lives in a linear fashion—we go, go, go and grab a sense of recovery only when we get a chance or if we can fit it in. Our society has become totally dysfunctional in how we live our lives. By understanding macrocycles and microcycles of recovery, we can balance stress and recovery and thrive in our lives instead of simply survive to get through each day and prepare for the next. Romans 12:2 tells us, *Do not conform any longer to the pattern of this world, but be transformed by the renewing of your mind.*

Q: *In your book,* The Corporate Athlete, *you state, "Without spiritual energy, we are nothing." Describe how spiritual energy transformed your pressure (negative thoughts) into power.*

A: The spiritual aspect of who you are is the most significant part of the puzzle. I was raised in a home where I was taught the only way to be successful was to achieve and get it done no matter what. Work until you drop and don't ever let up. Well, I believe I had achievement addiction as an adult. I was living of the world and for the world. I was raised in a Christian home but didn't really connect with my faith. I didn't realize that I could actually have a relationship with God, through His Son. It took a near-death experience for me to stop, listen, and feel that God was constantly working and loved me unconditionally. No matter how badly I messed things up, He still loved me and accepted me for who I was. Today, my viewpoint is well said by Colossians 3:23: *Whatever you do, work at it with all your heart, as working for the Lord, not for men.*

Q: *In terms of helping people transform negative stress into positive power and maximum performance, what practical advice can you give?*

A: First, ask yourself whom you are trying to please—the world, other people, or God? Second, if you're negative in any way, you have already received that feedback, perhaps from a family member, a friend, or a colleague. When you feel yourself going negative, say "Stop" and ask yourself, What matters most right now? Do this over and over and you will be amazed at how your life will transform.

Counsel for Consideration

Come to me, all you who are weary and burdened, and I will give you rest. Take my yoke upon you and learn from me, for I am gentle and humble in heart, and you will find rest for your souls. For my yoke is easy and my burden is light.

—Matthew 11:28–30

Pressure consumes a large percentage of our energy. Leaders can easily become weary and burdened. Jack Groppel confirmed, "We typically work and live our lives in linear fashion—we go, go, go and grab a sense of recovery only when we get a chance or if we can fit it in." We go when it's time to rest, take charge when it's best to surrender, and focus on our strengths and avoid our weaknesses when we would be far more effective by confronting the blind spots that betray our strengths.

The Four A's—the steps for transforming pressure into power—are modeled after David not because of his reputation as a courageous leader but because of his intimacy with God. He was yoked with God. As a leader, he knew when to take charge and when to surrender, when to act and when to rest.

Over time, the creative tension between David and the Lord resulted in a man who continued to lead, but who also grew to experience rest. Therefore, the Bible provides word pictures of David as both the no-holds-barred leader and as one who was able to relinquish his controlling behaviors and allow God to lead. In those times, David rested in God's power. *He makes me lie down in green pastures, he leads me beside quiet waters, he restores my soul* (Psalm 23:2–3). *Be still before the Lord and wait patiently for him* (Psalm 37:7). This Type A leader began to use different words—*be still, wait patiently, He makes me lie down*—all showing the importance of resting in the Lord.

Spiritual rest is as important a recovery tool as physical or emotional rest. Sometimes we simply have to trust Jesus when He says, *Come to me and I will give you rest.*

I know that God's wisdom is unconventional and often counterintuitive to society's expectations and our own thinking. It's one thing to know how to transform pressure into power; it's quite another to do it. Accepting your shortcomings, overcoming your fears, relinquishing control and subordinating your will to God, and being still and waiting are perhaps the most difficult things you'll ever do. It will take every bit of faith, courage, discipline, and perseverance you can muster. Allow me to encourage you in Jesus' own words: *I tell you the truth, if you have faith as small as a mustard seed, you can say to this mountain, 'Move from here to there' and it will move. Nothing is impossible for you.*

6

Pace

The Gift of Grace
to Run Your Race

Issue: How Can I Keep from Being Overwhelmed by Urgent Work Demands?

ive minutes into the strategic planning session, I sensed something was terribly wrong. I had been hired to facilitate a strategic planning session for an up-and-coming medical device company. Sitting around the table were seven business executives who, despite their youth, were showing signs of burnout and extreme fatigue.

Just eight months prior, five of these leaders made a decision to double the size of their company in order to speed the introduction of an innovative device into the marketplace. In order to beat the competition to the punch, however, they were forced to pick up the pace considerably—they would be running at a sprinter's pace for more than a year. Just over halfway into the timeline, fatigue was jeopardizing both the life of the company and the lives of those working for the company.

This dilemma belonged to a group of good and decent leaders who desired to honor God and do the right thing. Their mission was honorable—their product will save lives. On the other hand, however, they chose to gain a competitive advantage by assuming a sprinter's pace.

I was concerned about their risk of burnout due to the fast and furious pace. I really wonder whose race they were running. In the end, what's the right pace? How can a leader run at his or her God-given pace yet keep from being overwhelmed by urgent work demands?

Solution: Run Your Race at Your God-given Pace

Let us run with perseverance the race marked out for us.

—Hebrews 12:1

Counseling us to "run with perseverance the race marked out for us," the Apostle Paul makes two bold statements. He tells us to run the race uniquely *marked out for us* and he tells us to *run with perseverance.* Perseverance is persisting in spite of counterinfluences, opposition, or discouragement.

As I attempted to apply this counsel to my clients, I understood both the truth in Paul's message and how counterintuitive the statement is to today's conventional wisdom. How does conventional wisdom affect us? My clients felt they had no choice but to sprint with all they had in order to outpace the competition. Business leaders, faced with demands from every side (customers, shareholders, suppliers, and employees), feel the need to work longer, harder, and more efficiently. Leaders can't really be sure whether they've done enough.

In this chapter, you'll discover that God cares more about how you produce your best effort under difficult circumstances than the outcome. Conventional wisdom can easily blind us into running the wrong race at the wrong pace. God's wisdom counsels us to run the race marked out for us in spite of all the opposition and discouragement we face. In order to run with perseverance, we need to understand our personal pace. Discovering the pace God has gifted you with will help guide you on your path through uncertainty.

Discover the Gift of Grace to Run Your Race

God has blessed each of us with a certain rate at which we naturally navigate through life, just as He's blessed us with different personalities, roles, and forms of intelligence and senses of humor, among other characteristics. One pace isn't better than another—they're just different.

Once again, however, life is messy. Our lives provide a dynamic, ever-changing set of circumstances that demand our response. Rapid change requires our rapid response. It may mean we need to speed up our pace to keep up with the demands of the moment. At other times, we need to slow down and allow change to occur at an almost unperceivable rate. In either extreme, the flow of change can easily take us off our natural, God-given pace—the rate at which God designed us to move through life.

Let's revisit the dilemma faced by the young executives at the medical device company. These leaders sincerely desire to serve God by being the best they can be in service to others. On one hand, temporarily increasing their pace to get their product to market seems like a wise and legitimate decision. On the other hand, by choosing a sprinter's pace, they risk being a less effective steward of their gifts and responsibilities as leaders. How, then, are we to run our race?

Three Questions to Help Pace Your Race

1. What's Your Pace?

God uniquely designed and calibrated each of us with a natural pace at which we move through life. Our rates of progress through life aren't measured by one standard, but by a standard unique to each of us. Why? Because our pace is a reflection of the person God designed us to be.

We learn in the Parable of the Talents (Matthew 25:14–30) that

God is less concerned with our accomplishments and more concerned about how we're accomplishing within our unique capacity. God was equally joyful when the man with two talents produced two more as when the man with five talents produced five more. Furthermore, the parable tells us, *After a long time, the master of those servants returned.* This implies that God wasn't looking for an immediate return, but understood that they were producing the talents at their own unique pace.

I'll rely on the classic tale "The Turtle and the Hare" for this discussion. While we may not fall neatly into one category or the other, the familiarity of the story will help us discover our place on the pace continuum.

Are you a hare? Hares are built for speed and thrive on a fast pace. They have a high capacity to do many things within a short amount of time. Hares process and make decisions quickly. CEOs, stockbrokers, and emergency room physicians are commonly hares.

Are you a turtle? In addition to being slow and methodical, turtles are generally more cautious than hares. (Being a turtle myself, I'm all too familiar with their characteristics.) Turtles need time to research, analyze data, and think through problems. Turtles are typically suited for professions such as architects, researchers, and artists. They thrive in situations where they have time to think, analyze decisions, and create.

Again, what's important isn't whether we're a turtle or a hare but how we run our race. Let's take a closer look at the potential opportunities and threats of each pace and how to recalibrate our tempo to adjust to life's changes.

The Hare

Catherine's ambitions were matched only by her energy. Her life included a part-time job as director of human resources, some consulting work on the side, volunteering at her church, going to graduate school to earn her master's degree in organizational development, and being a mom to three daughters aged seven, eleven, and fourteen. Catherine worked best when the pace was fast and multifaceted, achieving whatever she set out to do.

When Catherine's employer eliminated her part-time position, she quickly responded with multiple strategies. She sought to increase her consulting hours, added to her class load, and began a hunt for a new part-time human resources position. A tribute to her talent, each of her strategies worked. Catherine's new position required more hours. The consulting project she picked up required another handful of hours. On top of that, she had to work extra hours in the evening when she added a class to her already busy schedule.

It quickly became evident to Catherine that old ladies who drive their Buicks to church on Sundays don't burn out their engines. She, on the other hand, was in danger of doing just that. Race cars may be built for speed, but they break down and burn out faster than a Sunday Buick. Catherine's pace became her undoing. She became less effective in every area of her life.

Hares have a tendency to run ahead of God. Catherine worked at the pace that came easiest for her: full throttle. In our coaching process, we agreed that she was trying to accomplish more than God intended and that by adjusting her pace to her God-given one she could focus more on what was truly important. We discovered that her need for control was the primary issue. When difficulty came her way, she felt she could control the situation by putting her foot on the gas pedal. She perceived going slower as a weakness; it meant she was lazy. Catherine was raised to be the best and felt that if more was better, then the faster you are, the better you are. Through a process of discovering what God intended for her, Catherine learned how to lift her foot off the gas pedal to keep her at her God-given pace. She made some hard decisions to deliberately slow down her rate of progress toward her goals. In the end, her new pace proved to help her regain her effectiveness.

The Turtle

Bill loved his job as head of accounting and finance for a small engineering firm—it was slow, steady, and predictable. He could look ahead and know exactly what his weekly, monthly, quarterly, and annual goals were. He knew when he would be busy and when he could plan a vacation.

Life changed dramatically when a large company bought out his firm. The pace changed as quickly as the expectations. The new organization had a reputation for growth and conducted business with more efficiency. They asked Bill to streamline his accounting procedures and to be more flexible and accommodating with employees. Each new expectation came with a new deadline.

Bill's response? He slowed down, reverting to the pace at which he was most comfortable. He felt he needed to get a handle on the changes and analyze the best way to streamline the old procedures. He needed time to respond properly to employees' demands and to assimilate to the expectations placed on him. Unfortunately, his peers and associates didn't have time to wait for Bill to get his act together. Frictions grew and Bill was perceived as the wrench in the engine of progress. The greater the friction grew, the more Bill hunkered down.

As I worked with him, I respected Bill's God-given pace but also needed to help him work through his two choices: He could adjust his tempo to the new environment or find another job with a pace that better suited him. We discovered that lack of confidence and lack of control were two of the issues that kept him from responding to the needs of others. Bill recognized that his desire to do things perfectly slowed him down. His need for time alone to figure things out kept him from being a part of his new team. The more his responsibilities seemed out of his control, the more he tried to take control by shutting himself away and putting his foot on the brake.

Turtles have a tendency to lag behind God's pace. They are loyal and excellent workers who need space and time to produce quality work, but there are also times when they need a fair amount of encouragement and prodding. On a personal level, Bill recalibrated his pace by trusting more in his abilities and letting go of perfectionist tendencies. On an interpersonal level, we held partnering meetings between Bill and his associates. We were able to clarify roles, responsibilities, and expectations. His associates gained a better understanding of how Bill works best, and Bill took the steps necessary to increase his pace.

Ironically, while Bill and Catherine are built differently, they have one thing in common: They each want to be in control of their respective pace. In each situation, they partnered with God to adjust their pace. Catherine took a leap of faith by easing her foot off the pedal. Bill courageously took his foot off the brake and put it on the gas pedal. By relinquishing control of the issues that impacted their respective paces and adjusting to their situations, they actually gained control.

Do all hares need to slow down and all turtles need to speed up? Absolutely not. What I'm advocating is discovering your God-given pace and being true to that. Play to your strengths, but don't let your strengths play you. In other words, be aware of the issues that may hide in your strength. Catherine identified issues that made her go faster when going slower was best. In adjusting to a slower pace, she still remained a hare (i.e., her strength). Bill remained a turtle, but adjusted to his situation from a position of strength.

Remember, pace isn't a matter of how fast or slow you're going, but your rate of progress and manner of walking as you journey through life. God has uniquely marked out a race for you to run. He desires that you grow with every twist, turn, and fork on the path. Use every change and new circumstances you face to recalibrate your pace to run your race.

2. Whose Race Are You Running?

One of my first jobs was as a busboy in a restaurant known for its frenetic lunchtimes. The waiters literally sprinted with food orders from tables to the kitchen and back to tables with hot meals in hand. It was a well-paying summer job with one drawback: I was a turtle working in a hare environment. As fast as I moved, I was still too slow for the job. After a particularly busy lunch rush, the maître d' called me over and politely said, "Larry, you're a great kid with a great work ethic, but you're just too slow for this job. We're going to have to let you go."

One would think I would get the message. What did I do? Upon graduation from college, I entered the hotel and restaurant industry, one of the fastest-paced careers one can pursue. Why would anyone do such a thing?

First, I believed I could win any race I set my mind to. I refused to believe that I was too slow for any job. I was taught that I could be whatever I put my effort into. I was told to focus on my strengths and not my weaknesses. I was never taught to consider what I was good at versus what I wasn't. My ego got in the way. As a result, my pride prompted me to pursue the wrong race. I pursued a specific career path for all the wrong reasons.

Second, I was focused more on the prize than on the race. As I entered the hospitality industry, my eyes were fixed on quick advancement, a glamorous lifestyle, and financial opportunity rather than the career itself. For me, the end justified the means.

Third, I focused on getting a head start on my classmates. Like most college graduates, I was competing for an opportunity to get my career started. My uncle was successful and well connected in the hotel business. I figured if I chose hotel management I would have a good shot at getting a head start and beating the competition. My strategy worked. Through a series of political favors, I was able to get a position as a corporate trainee at a major hotel corporation.

Fast-forward thirteen years into my career. It was a typical day for the sales and marketing director of a large luxury hotel. As usual, I was at work by 6:00 A.M. to try to lower my inbox to a manageable level before the frenetic pace of my twelve-hour day kicked in. By 10:12 A.M. I was in full swing. I had already attended an executive committee meeting, conducted a sales meeting, and met with a client from New York, and I was on my way to the catering office to put out the first of several fires that needed to be handled ASAP.

As I scurried to the catering office, I glanced over and saw the general manager standing in front of his office. He looked at me and said, "Larry, can I see you in my office for a minute?" Following me in, he closed the door and softly said, "Larry, we're going to have to let you go."

For thirteen years, I sprinted from quarter to quarter, running the wrong race for the wrong reasons. On the surface, my rationale certainly coincided with conventional wisdom. *You can be whatever you want to be. Seize the opportunity before you. Win the race.* The flaw in all this "wisdom" is that it was never the race marked out for *me*.

I was lucky in that the decision to leave one race and pursue another was made for me—I had no choice in the matter. I eventually started my own business in leadership development and through many other twists and turns became an author. I still live in a hare world, but my job now is perfectly suited for my turtle gifts. I can spend hours investing in the activities necessary to write, such as research, prayer, and reflection.

I know I'm not alone in running someone else's race. One client's race was determined by a parent's expectation. Another CEO frantically ran at a pace determined by a significant stakeholder's quarterly profit expectations. I know of a company of 250 employees who raced to get a new product to market before their primary competitor. In each of these cases, the race was determined by an outside influence and someone's erroneous beliefs rather than God's call.

Every dead end has a new beginning. What a relief that was to me. I hope it's also an encouragement to those who've been running the wrong race or feel their race has come to a dead end. Maybe you feel it's too late to change careers. Perhaps joining the race God has marked out for you is accompanied by financial risk. Take heart. God designed us to grow until we die. With God, new life springs from death. Every dead end creates a doorway to a new beginning. Shortsighted thinking may tell you you're at a dead end and have lost the race. That's a lie from the pit of hell. God wastes nothing; He uses everything for His glory. God sees the big picture and knows your potential. Your old race was simply a training ground for the new race that lies ahead.

3. What's the Prize?

At fifty-six, Big John was the ideal salesperson—larger than life and loved by employees and customers alike. He looked like a cross between Santa Claus and Paul Bunyan: six-foot-three and 260 pounds of booming voice and presence. You knew when Big John walked into the room. He had tons of energy, loved people, loved a party, and was highly goal driven. When it came to his short-term business goals, he was a master. He was either the top sales producer or among the top producers for the previous fifteen years. When it came to his long-term goal of running a fishing camp for underprivileged kids, he was on "someday isle." Every year, Big John would write down the same New Year's resolutions: (1) Start a diet and exercise program; (2) spend more time at home with the kids; and (3) start making plans for Big John's Fish Camp.

As important as his resolutions were to him, the years came and went without their achievement. Big John's employer took advantage of his skills by creating powerful motivation. His liberal expense account included entertainment at the finest restaurants and clubs in the country. He was rewarded with bonuses for sales in excess of his quarterly and annual goals. The organization drove its sales staff hard. There was no room for mediocrity. You either produced or you were bounced to the curb. As good as Big John was, he was always looking over his shoulder at the new guys. On the surface, he laughed at the good-natured ribbing that said he was slowing down. In reality, he hid the stress that came from knowing he needed to prove himself continually to compete and keep his job.

> *For a man is a slave to whatever has mastered him.*
>   —2 Peter 2:19

Sadly, Big John passed away one winter evening of a heart attack. Maybe it was his excess weight, maybe it was his smoking, or maybe it was the stress of the job. We don't know exactly what happened; we only know that Big John was mastered by a very powerful set of short-term motivations.

Our short-term rewards can take us off our God-given race and our God-given pace. Two powerful short-term motivators work in tandem to take us off our God-given path: one from the outside and one from within. While Big John was incented by external rewards ("carrots" like expense accounts and financial rewards, and "sticks" such as the pressure to produce), even more powerful were his internal impulses. Big John was a slave to immediate gratification. He loved the good life; he loved smoking, drinking, and eating good food with friends and clients.

Together, these rewards provided motivation that was practically impossible to overcome. His liberal expense account and sales incentives legitimized his reasons for eating and drinking. After all, he was doing this to produce sales, succeed in business, and provide for his family. Deep down, however, Big John became a slave to instant gratification and was taken out of his God-given race and pace.

Place your purpose over pressure, pleasure, and pride. Big John's story, while extreme, is common. We each face an ongoing battle between our immediate desires and our long-term purpose. We may desire long-term health and longevity yet face the immediate temptation of a chocolate cake. Our dreams are forced to take a backseat (again) to the demands of the present. Our long-term business vision takes a backseat to the needs of the current quarter.

Nothing will get you out of your God-given race and off your God-given pace faster than pressure, pleasure, and pride. They will speed you up, slow you down, or derail you altogether. To deny their presence is to take the approach of the ostrich that hides his head in the ground while standing among the pack of hungry lions.

Realistically, the human motivations of pleasure, fear, pain avoidance, achievement, power, money, and security are much more powerful than we care to admit. What's the solution? How can we live with the delayed gratification of our long-term mission when we're driven by such a powerful need for immediate self-gratification? Helen Keller, who faced as much adversity as most of us will ever know, once said, "Many persons have a wrong idea of what constitutes real happiness. It's not obtained through self-gratification, but through fidelity to a worthy purpose."

The more you understand and strengthen your God-given purpose, the less you'll be a slave to pressure, pleasure, and pride. Earlier in this book, I asked, Are you a consumer or a catalyst? If you have a consumer mentality, you'll be a slave to immediate gratification and never be satisfied. With a catalyst mentality, you'll embrace your role as serving God's greater purpose. King Solomon allowed pressure, pleasure, and pride to overtake his purpose. He speaks with authority when he states in Ecclesiastes, *All of men's efforts are for his mouth yet his appetite is never satisfied.*

In Ecclesiastes 3, Solomon describes how serving God's purpose is ultimately a gift of God and the only means for finding true happiness and satisfaction. *I have seen the burden God has laid on men. He has made everything beautiful in its time. He has also set eternity in the hearts of men; yet they cannot fathom what God has done from beginning to end. I know that there is nothing better for men than to be happy and do good while they live. That every man may eat and drink, and find satisfaction in all his toil—this is the gift of God.*

Mentor on a Mission

Geoff Miller is the mental skills coach for the Pittsburgh Pirates and a partner at Winning Mind, LLC, a San Diego–based high-performance consulting group. Winning Mind works with elite performers in Fortune 500 companies, professional and amateur sports, and Special Forces units of the military.

Geoff understands the rewards and pressures of winning. In cultures where winning is everything, such as sports and business, Geoff's insights are both insightful and practical. His sports analogies will help you discover how to win your race, in business and in life. Here are his insights and comments.

Q: What key pitfalls impact winning or losing?

A: At the highest levels in sports, mental factors are the difference between winning and losing. Losing focus is a key pitfall. The ability to stay focused on your purpose and your plan is a key element of winning your race.

Q: In a recent article in Peak Running Performance, *you gave a radical formula for winning. Please explain it.*

A: Winning, whether in sports or achieving success in your own personal and professional race, is about producing your best effort, not about an outcome.

Q: How does this definition sit with highly driven people where winning affirms that they've produced their best effort?

A: This is the toughest thing for very competitive people to do. If they do their best, they feel they should win. If they lose, they feel they should have done more to win.

What I do is work backwards with these individuals. I tell them, "If you did your best and you did everything you could do today, and you still didn't win, don't you have to be okay with that? What else could you have done?"

Q: If success isn't necessarily winning the race, how do you define success?

A: Success is knowing that you've done all you could to run your race and being okay with whatever the outcome is because there's nothing else you could have done.

Q: We live in business environments where winning drives our lives. How can highly competitive people break out of that trap?

A: Many athletes get so consumed with their competitors they forget about what they themselves are doing. At the core, it's an issue of control.

To bring them back in focus, I ask, "Are you competing with the person across the net or giving your best effort?" Another way to ask the question is, "Can you be okay with just doing what you have control over?"

Winning isn't really about an outcome. It's about a process. If winning really were the only thing, what would be the harm in cheating? When you think about it, doesn't the feeling you get when you win come just as much from knowing how hard you worked for it, as it does from knowing how much you wanted it? Highly competitive people need to remember that it's not just winning that they are after.

Q: Control is an issue for most people. Explain further how control translates into success.

A: Talented businesspeople and athletes waste precious energy on things they can't control. A great quarterback can't control how much time his offensive line gives him to throw the ball. A figure skater has no control over how the judging panel will score her performance. Runners have no control over the conditions in which they run.

When winning is your main concern, these variables can pose great distractions. They don't seem so daunting when you focus on doing your best regardless of who or what you're up against. The bottom line is this: You have a better chance of winning if you simply focus on giving your best effort rather than setting out to take first place.

Counsel for Consideration

Geoff Miller asserts that the only thing we can control is doing our best. I concur that winning our race and being successful is about producing our best effort and not the outcome. I can't help, though, but ask the question, What does it mean to do our best?

There are days where I really struggle with that question. Am I being the best husband I can be? The best parent? Am I doing my best at work? Am I honoring God with my best? What's the scorecard that measures and affirms whether I'm doing my best? I must admit that, since such a scorecard doesn't exist, some nights when my head hits the pillow I reflect on the day and wonder, I worked hard but did I really accomplish anything?

I imagine I'm not alone—most of us are looking for some reward or affirmation for our efforts. Those around us may seek that reward from pleasure, winning, status, possessions, financial security, or praise. The concept of running our race with perseverance, then, is counterintuitive. In essence, it means doing your best without immediate affirmation or reward. It means waiting when you feel pressured to act. Being patient when you have no patience. Taking a leap of faith when it doesn't make earthly sense.

Driving home from the strategic planning session with my young business clients, I felt like a hypocrite. Their immediate reaction to a competitor's clinical trial and some deceitful actions was to take charge of the race and pick up the pace yet again. I advised these leaders that the right way to take control of the situation was to be the best leaders they could be and not allow their competitor's actions to dictate the race. This also meant surrendering things outside of their control to God. I said "insightful" things like, "Just do your best and trust the outcome to God," and "Forgive your enemy," and "Overcome evil with good." As I drove home that day, however, I asked myself what I would do in that situation. Would I take my own advice? I didn't know if I could do it—it simply seemed like too big a leap of faith.

So here I persist in giving you the same advice I provided for my clients, knowing you will find it to be difficult and counter-intuitive, but sharing it with you because I know it's right. If you're a turtle, you may need to speed up. If you're a hare, you may need to slow down. Search out your God-given race when you feel stuck in someone else's race. Pursue delayed gratification over immediate gratification.

It may seem impractical and impossible to run your race with perseverance. It takes great courage, patience, and perseverance to do your best when there are no immediate rewards that affirm you're doing so. Sometimes, running your race can feel like a long and painful marathon with no finish line in sight. Sometimes, God is waiting for you to let go of one race so you can run a new race, one uniquely marked out for you. Sometimes doing your best means trusting that God has a race uniquely designed for you and choosing to run with perseverance until you discover it.

Taking Control by Surrendering Control: The Art of Giving Yourself a Break

For whoever wants to save his life will lose it, but whoever loses his life for me will find it.

—Matthew 16:25

Schindler's List tells the story of Oskar Schindler, the German businessman who was instrumental in saving the lives of Polish Jews who were otherwise doomed to die in Nazi concentration camps. Schindler's List refers to the list of 1,100 Jews whom, by hiring them to work in his factory and persuading and bribing Nazi officers, were kept from death at the hands of Nazis.

In the closing scenes, the German army surrenders and Schindler, now broke from paying to save the Jews, must flee the oncoming Soviet Red Army. His car is packed and he says good-bye to the Jewish workers he saved from death. To thank him, the workers give him a ring engraved with the Talmudic quotation *He who saves the life of one man, saves the world entire.* Seeing his luxury car, Schindler is consumed with guilt, realizing he could have used it to save ten more people. Panged with regret for not having done more, he breaks down in tears.

Did Schindler feel he had done his best? Did he feel like a success? No. Schindler cried because he felt he could have done more. Today, the descendants of the Schindler Jews now number over seven thousand! Over *seven thousand people and counting* are making an impact on the world because Oskar Schindler did his best under agonizing circumstances.

Many of us have felt like Schindler. We think that our best can be better. In truth, however, God joyfully embraces our best. He asks for nothing more. If you're the type of leader who's willing to invest time in a book like this, you're likely a hardworking leader who seeks to do all you can for God's glory. Sometimes we just need to give ourselves a break. Hardworking people often find it difficult to rest; they feel that rest keeps them from doing their best. Rest means *trusting in God's strength* so you can be your best. Paul provides great insight when he says: *I have learned the secret of being content in any and every situation, whether well fed or hungry, whether living in plenty or in want. I can do everything through him who gives me strength* (Philippians 4:12–13). If you've sought God's wisdom and given your best toward your noble pursuit in partnership with God, then you can rest knowing you're running your race at your God-given pace.

A good friend of mine once confessed, "Sometimes my life feels like I have one foot on the gas and one foot on the brake." The balance between control and surrender, ambition and contentment, and work and rest challenges the best of us. I encourage you to think of these not as conflicting ideals but as complementary attributes. Each attribute is a gift of God. Without its complementary attribute, however, any one of them will lead us off our God-given race and pace. Work without rest, for example, is burnout. Rest without work is laziness.

In His grace, God has designed into the depths of our being an amazing system of not just checks and balances, but synergy. Our internal gas pedal and brake are unique to each of us. Together, they work in harmony so we can follow the race God has marked out for us at our God-given pace. Paul's counsel in Philippians reveals our internal synergy. By surrendering our present tempo we gain control of our God-given pace. By recognizing a dead end, a new beginning is revealed. By breaking the bondage of short-term rewards we gain the satisfaction of a long-term purpose. Ultimately, by surrendering control of our lives, we can run with perseverance the race marked out for us.

So if you're a hare, remember to use the brake every once in a while. If you're a turtle, don't be afraid to use the gas pedal. If you're not sure whose race you're running, search out and discover the race God has marked out for you. Focus your eyes on your purpose and, finally, give your best and trust God with the rest. By discovering your God-given pace, may you receive the gift of grace to run your race and the blessing of clarity in an uncertain world.

7

Place

The Gift of Your Environment

Issue: What's the Best Work Environment for Me?

The most frequently asked question I receive is posed one of two ways: Either *How do I find the best work environment for me?* or *Should I stay or should I go?* The heart of the letter typically reads something like this:

> I presently work at _____. While the company provides a good salary and benefits package, I find myself losing motivation. I feel like my talents aren't being fully utilized. I'm concerned with the lack of integrity from our senior leadership. There are times where I feel like I'm being forced to compromise my values in order to do my job.
>
> Ideally, I'd like to stay if conditions improve but I'm not confident that will happen. Should I stick with my job and do my best under the circumstances or should I go and seek a better work environment with a more ethical culture? Do you have a list of companies with good ethics and values? I certainly would enjoy working in that type of environment.

I appreciate the heart from which this question is asked. There's nothing wrong with seeking an ethical work culture that aligns with our values. While finding a good environment is important, however, it may not be the *right* environment.

What's the best question we can ask ourselves? *Is this environment good or bad? Should I stay or should I go? What's the best work environment for me?* Or is there an even better question?

Solution: Be in the Right Place at the Right Time

And who knows but that you have come to royal position for such a time as this?

—Esther 4:14

Esther was a young Jewish woman chosen to be queen to Xerxes, King of Persia. Esther neither chose her new position nor desired the circumstances thrust upon her. Shortly after her appointment, her cousin, Mordecai, became aware that King Xerxes' second-in-command was secretly plotting to destroy all the Jews in Persia. Pleading with Esther to reveal the plot to the king while knowing it would put her life in danger, Mordecai implores Esther with the powerful words of Esther 4:14.

Esther was in the right place at the right time: a moment where environment and circumstances interact with one individual's spirit to create a significant impact. Fortunately, she was also in the right place spiritually, as she had the moral courage and wisdom necessary for the situation. God placed Esther in her environment so that she might be instrumental in saving the Jews of Persia. Esther understood that the opportunity was God-given and seized it.

The best question we can ask ourselves is neither *Is this environment good or bad?* nor *Should I stay or should I go?* The best question we can ask is this: *Am I in the right place at the right time?* I believe God has placed you, like Esther, in a royal position in order to play an important role in others' lives. In this chapter, we'll discover that environments aren't either good or bad or right or wrong. Sometimes being placed in an environment at a specific time brings out the best in us so that we can bring out the best in our environment.

Discover the Gift of Your Environment

How do you know when you've discovered your right place? The right place isn't necessarily a specific physical location, nor is it necessarily a good environment. The right place is a place in time where your environment impacts you and you impact your environment. In essence, the right place is where your environment brings out the best in you so you can bring out the best in others.

The messages around us tell us to avoid bad environments that diminish our skills and find a good environment that best utilizes our skills. While it appears to be good advice, this one-dimensional thinking falls short of God's path and purpose for you.

The word *place* has three definitions. Place can be defined as 1.) an external physical environment; 2.) an internal state of mind, as in *World War II vets are in a different place than today's youth;* or 3.) an appropriate moment in time, as in *This isn't the place to discuss compensation.* Each of the three dimensions is important but insufficient on its own. Combine them, however, and they interact to create a powerful "right place at the right time" opportunity. If we consider "place" as an equation, it would look like this:

Environment + State of Mind + Right Time = Significant Impact

Do you remember your third-grade science class and the amazing volcano experiment? Three relatively benign ingredients—dish soap, baking soda, and vinegar—are combined. The result is a volcano filled with fizzing, popping, crackling, and oozing "lava." The elements of the "right place at the right time" opportunity are similar; when aligned and allowed to interact, they have the potential to create a significant impact. Let's take a look at each of the three elements.

Environment

Our environment provides the trigger that sparks the best (and the worst) in us.

Environment is the circumstances or conditions that surround us. This includes physical circumstances such as a workplace (perhaps a cubicle, a downtown high-rise office, a highway, or a mail route). Environment can also be defined in terms of relationships. This can include a specific relationship such as with a boss or co-worker, or it can describe how you're influenced by a culture such as a business or community.

The right environment is the one that triggers the best in us, a place where our unique passions, purpose, and giftedness come alive. To an artist, it may be a snow-capped mountain at sunset that motivates him to paint for hours on end. To an employee, it may be a word of praise from a boss that motivates him to work an extra hour to complete a project. To a psychologist, it may be the emotional pain of a client that motivates her to research a solution.

The conditions within which we work and live will either activate and motivate our unique giftedness or deactivate or discourage our giftedness. Let's look at two examples.

Marianne was a successful salesperson who loved her job. She loved being on the road and serving her customers. Following her promotion to sales director, she moved to the home office to train and manage salespeople. While this was a promotion in status and pay, her new environment no longer motivated her. Marianne floundered in her job and eventually left. What happened? The triggers in her environment changed, both the physical location and her relationships with others. This shift in environment diminished the triggers that motivated her natural giftedness.

Paul worked as a meeting planner for a large company. His job was to manage all the details that went into creating a successful meeting, including finding hotel accommodations, booking speakers, and coordinating travel arrangements. One day, a scheduled speaker became ill and had to cancel. Finding no last-minute alternative, Paul was forced to fill in and speak on leadership, something he was passionate about. He was a hit! This exciting and satisfying experience inspired Paul to work toward a new career. Over time, he became an accomplished and successful speaker. While good at organizing details to create successful meetings, Paul discovered that he was great at organizing thoughts into successful speeches. The same innate gifts used in a new environment (both conditions and people) triggered a very different passion.

As we discovered in Chapter 1, "Purpose: The Gift of Your Unique Calling," both the physical conditions and the relationships within our environment play key roles in activating our giftedness. It's not sufficient, then, simply to understand the culture of an organization and its values. We must also explore the *kinds* of conditions and the *nature* of relationships that bring out our best. It is, therefore, incumbent upon us to ask, What triggers my motivation? What sustains my drive when conditions turn bad? What types of relationships motivate me? What kind of culture brings out my best? What kinds of relationships or cultures inhibit my growth?

Your environment can bring out your best or worst. It can lead you to significance or render you insignificant. Regardless of whether you're seeking a new environment or staying in your existing environment, don't allow the wrong circumstances to determine your fate. Rather, seek the right circumstances that trigger your best. In the end, ensure that you're in the environment that brings out the best in you so you can bring out the best in others.

State of Mind

Your state of mind determines how you respond to your environment.
God's first question to Adam was posed after he sinned. "Where

are you?" God asked. Adam responded, "The woman you put here
with me—she gave me some fruit from the tree, and I ate it." When
God asked, "Where are you?" however, He wasn't inquiring as to
Adam's location; he was delving into Adam's state of mind. Your environment is important but will be rendered irrelevant if you're not
in the right state of mind. There are leaders throughout the world
who are in the right environment but in the wrong place emotionally and spiritually. Distractions, from pursuit of power to the pressure to perform, threaten to impact our state of mind negatively.

Some of my clients have desired new environments for all the
wrong reasons. One, for example, felt that a new environment would
solve his problems, but his state of mind was such that he would not
be able to find the right place at the right time in even the most
perfect environment.

Joyfully, I also know leaders who do remarkable and significant
things in spite of an environment you or I would be tempted to label
as "bad." Their state of mind transcends whatever challenge comes
before them.

Where are you? Regardless of your environment, if your mind-
set isn't in the right place, you'll miss your right-place-at-the-right-
time opportunity.

Right Time

The appropriate moment determines the right time and the right place.

Timing plays a key role in determining the right place at the
right time. Is timing just dumb luck? Is it a matter of odds, like winning the lottery? In God's economy, no! Being in the right place at
the right time may seem the opposite of that exciting moment when
one realizes he's won the lottery. It may come during a time period
that is mundane, boring, and even discouraging. God may have you
in a time of waiting, growth, training, and preparation.

During my years of drudgery trying to write *God Is My CEO*
and find a publisher, I thought I was in the wrong place at the wrong

time. I constantly questioned God's timing. I felt stuck in an environment and state of mind that showed no tangible evidence of success. After *God Is My CEO* was published (finally), one woman asked, "How did you work the timing of your book—coming out right at the time of the corporate scandals?" Drudgery, daily mundane routine, and total discouragement had been paired with God's perfect timing.

We live in a fast-paced world that waits for no one. We tend to jump at opportunities. Solomon states in Ecclesiastes 3:1, *There is a time for everything, and a season for every activity under heaven.* Some moments call for immediate action. Other times are heavy with waiting and preparation. Regardless, we're called to be ready. In order to be ready, we need to have a keen awareness of the appropriate time, environment, and state of mind as they come together to form the right place at the right time. Trust that God will reveal this unique moment in time to you. As Solomon reminds us in Ecclesiastes 3:11, *He has made everything beautiful in its time.*

Environment + State of Mind + Right Time = Significant Impact

The interaction of the elements produces significance.

I'm excited to share with you stories of three leaders from three environments. Each was in the right place at the right time. I believe the elements of environment, state of mind, and right time visibly interact and the significance of the interaction is evident.

Randall Zindler, CEO, Medair

Several years ago, I met the young and talented Randall Zindler, CEO of Medair. Medair's mission is to respond to human suffering in emergency and disaster situations all over the world. This includes providing medical assistance, food, water, and sanitation, and rebuilding roads, housing, schools, and attending to any other needs. My interpretation of Medair's mission (through my state of mind) is this: Medair employees risk their lives to go to the most hostile environments in the world in order to work in the worst conditions imaginable, experiencing the worst of human suffering through famine, slavery, starvation, and injustice. They work in places such as Uganda, Darfur, and the Democratic Republic of Congo.

Truthfully, as I listened to Randall, I silently questioned his motives. I thought, *Randall is a bright, talented guy who could have multiple opportunities to work in a first-class environment with all the perks. Any member of Medair's extensive medical staff could easily find a financially rewarding physician position in the location of their choosing. Why would anyone this bright and talented choose to work in such dangerous, discouraging, and depressing circumstances?*

Thankfully, Randall and the other Medair men and women are in different states of mind, both emotionally and spiritually. Their environment triggers something so deep within their spirit that they're able to transform the worst environment into the right place at the right time.

Randall's passionate description of Medair's values (compassion, dignity, faith, accountability, integrity, and hope) wasn't the typical jargon of a CEO looking for a positive PR spin. This is an organization that lives the values of Jesus Christ. Medair's values are brought to life in the story of Martha, an eleven-year-old girl in one of the warzones in which Medair works. (Note: In order to protect those involved, the identifying details of Martha's story have been changed.)

Martha's mother had died in childbirth and tribal militias had killed her father. At the age of eleven, Martha was raped by the same militia and found herself pregnant. Anna, a Medair medic, found Martha in a rural camp for displaced people. Martha was alone with no one to help her; her only relative was a mentally ill uncle who beat her.

Anna explained Martha's plight to the rest of the Medair team and they all agreed to respond. When it was time for her to give

birth, Anna brought Martha to the town where the Medair team
was based, which had better medical facilities. Through a most difficult and life-threatening childbirth, Martha gave birth to a healthy
baby boy. After the birth, Nadine, a local member of the Medair
team, brought Martha and her son into her home.

While they had saved the lives of Martha and her son, the Medair team knew the local people would view an eleven-year-old girl
who'd been raped and her bastard son with a harsh reality: their lives
would be considered cursed. The Medair staff believed otherwise.

Understanding that it was important to recognize the dignity
and worth of both Martha and her son, they asked local Medair staff
of the region's religion, "What would a high-ranking official like
the governor of the region do if his wife gave birth to a son?" It was
explained that the community would have an all-day feast with the
finest food and provisions. Medair staff proceeded to throw a large
celebration worthy of the child of a noble dignitary. During the
celebration, Fraser Bell, Medair's regional head, prayed in the name
of Jesus and named the baby Joseph, after the statement in Genesis,
"You intended to harm me, but God intended it for good."

I had the opportunity to talk to Fraser recently. I knew his team
had witnessed 200,000 refugees with stories as hopeless as Martha's.
Why, I wondered, had the Medair team gone above and beyond to
help one child in such a sea of despair?

He responded, "When you are serving tens of thousands of people who are suffering, it's easy to forget the dignity of the individual.
Yet they each have a name and a story of their own. You must stay
sensitive enough to respond to the needs of one person. Sometimes
this requires us to go beyond the normal boundaries of project plans
in order to deeply impact one life. The fact that you cannot do this
for everyone is not a sufficient reason to do it for no one."

My conversation with Fraser stirred my heart as I recalled the
story of the old man on the beach. Thousands of starfish washed
up on the shore through a freak storm. The old man was throwing

the starfish back one at a time when a little boy came along. Looking at the thousands of starfish lying around, he asked, "Why are you doing this; what difference is it going to make?" The old man looked down at the starfish he had just picked up and said, "Well, it makes a difference to this one."

John Turnipseed, Community Leader and Director, Center for Fathering

Only nine impressionable years old, John Turnipseed was in the wrong place at the wrong time. The place was Hubert's barbershop, an inner-city hangout for pimps, thugs, and drug dealers. The time was after school, sometime between the three-o'clock bell and ten-thirty at night, when his mom, who worked all day and attended school in the evening, got home.

Hubert's was a magnet to a young kid wanting to be successful in life. The environment provided all the training, education, and rewards needed to produce a violent gang leader. As John explains, "I gravitated to whatever was given to me. Being bullied [by an abusive father] was the worst experience of my life. It made me feel helpless. It made me feel like I was nothing. I hated who I was. Watching my dad abuse my mother and not being able to protect her made me feel I wasn't being a man.

"The environment at Hubert's gave me the solution to my problem. Getting high, carrying guns, and using violence to solve your problems made you a winner. I was a quick learner. I learned that violence gave me many rewards—from money to power to prestige. I became the biggest bully on the block. I used intimidation and fear as weapons to obtain status and prestige."

From childhood to adulthood, John's life was marked by violence and heartache. His life shifted between jail time and probation. Thanks to a series of people who cared, John learned about computer programming in jail and eventually landed a probation job as a computer-programming teacher. "For the first time in my life," John recalls, "I felt like somebody. My students called me Mr. Turnipseed. It was the first time I had a job other than thug or thief."

Old habits, however, die hard. While he seemed to be on the right path, John began to gamble heavily and lost a lot of money. To supplement his modest income, he began to steal. Behind the scenes, a local television news station was doing an investigative report on John's activities. Catching up with him at the school where he was teaching, the news crew confronted him. He ran upstairs to his office, locked the door, and cried uncontrollably. "I felt little again. I was trying to be a good person but here I was, again a thief. I called my mom and she just kept saying, 'John, turn it all over to Jesus. Just turn it all over to Jesus.' I started praying. I was pleading with Jesus to save me. It's hard to put into words; all I can say is that I felt this overwhelming sense that everything would be okay." As John recalls, "It was clearly the most profound, life-changing moment in my life."

John's state of mind changed. From that point forward and certainly not without difficulty, he slowly transformed his life. For the first time, John had a peace and purpose in life that had never previously existed. "God not only saved me, He took care of me. He placed a series of people in my life to help me get reestablished with my family, work, and the community."

Over time, John's mind-set changed from gang leader to community leader. The fear that fueled his motivation was slowly replaced by love. The pain that caused him to hurt others began to be used to help others. His sense of entitlement as a thug was replaced by a sense of purpose.

Today, John Turnipseed is a respected leader in his community and director of the Center for Fathering. His experiences combined with God's blessings and wisdom allow him to impact powerfully the very environment that had such a negative impact on him. The Center for Fathering offers parenting and male responsibility classes.

It also assists men in identifying job skills and creating résumés, and provides numerous resources to assist in employment.

Beyond his role as director, however, John impacts his environment with every aspect of his being. "My job is to be available to anyone in the community who is struggling. I provide one-on-one counseling to guys getting out of prison. I have an outreach to criminals. I provide them hope by being an example of someone who can go from a life of prison to a life of promise."

To understand better the importance of a transformed state of mind, I asked John why he stays in the environment that caused such pain and heartache in his life. "My ministry is in the dark," he responded. "I believe God equipped me for this dark environment. I believe that Jesus will win out in the darkness just like He won out in me. My purpose in life is to put our conscience back in our families. I tell them, 'We're not pimps, thugs, and whores; we're children of God.' I want to end the generations of violence among men and set a new standard for fathering and grandfathering.

"I feel totally blessed. For the first time in my life, I have love, respect, and a job. Even more important, to know that you've made a difference in the lives of families is a wonderful accomplishment and joy. To see a family operating again is a great joy. All you have to do is change one family because you know you've affected future generations forever."

Eric Pillmore, Senior Vice President of Corporate Governance, Tyco International

On June 3, 2002, Dennis Kozlowski unexpectedly resigned as CEO of Tyco International, Ltd. The next day, the *New York Times* reported that Kozlowski was the subject of a sales tax evasion investigation by the Manhattan district attorney's office, and Tyco joined the ranks of Worldcom and Enron as a symbol of corporate greed, unethical leadership, and abuse of power. From June 4 on, Tyco would experience unprecedented turmoil that would include a complete overhaul of leadership and a highly publicized trial that would expose Kozlowski's extravagant lifestyle of $2 million parties and $6,000 shower curtains.

In July 2002, the Tyco board chose Ed Breen, former president and COO at Motorola, to replace Kozlowski. Eric Pillmore was at dinner the night the news came over the wire that Breen, Eric's old boss from General Instrument, had accepted the CEO job. The next day, Eric called his old boss and said, "Congratulations, I'd like to join you!" Eric Pillmore was named senior vice president of corporate governance at Tyco, charged with the task of restoring an ethical culture to an environment decimated and demoralized by unethical leadership, scandal, and upheaval.

Eric explains why he was so interested in joining an environment in turmoil. "At the time I was working through a study of a book called *Experiencing God* by Henry Blackaby with my mentor, Mac McQuiston. In the book, Blackaby states, 'If you want to know and do God's will, find out where God is working and join him.' I felt that God called me to this environment. I felt that my past experiences working in challenging environments prepared me for Tyco. I wanted to help the 240,000 employees at Tyco, the significant majority of whom were hardworking, honest people who were in the wrong place at the wrong time. I felt we could help investors who had lost their life savings to recover their investment. On a larger scale, as corporate America was crumbling, I saw a need for truth and clarity around values in business."

Whether it was fate, bad luck, or God's training and development plan, Eric had previously found himself mired in three successive unethical business environments where his core values had been challenged. In each environment, there was great pressure put on Eric to conform to the unethical culture. With this pressure came tremendous stress. As Eric explains, "The temptation to look the other way and just move on was great. That would have been the easiest and safest thing to do. However, I felt an obligation to expose the truth; I chose to make each situation transparent. Without pointing fingers at people, I wanted to lay out the truth of what was happening because that's the way we learn. The biggest value in crises is the learning."

Along with Tyco's new leadership team and board, Eric set out to restore an ethical culture to a culture negatively impacted by previous leadership. In a relatively short time, Tyco went from having the lowest possible global ratings (as measured in December 2002 by GovernanceMetrics International) to one of the highest (September 2005). In September 2006, Tyco received a perfect "10," placing it in the top 20 of America's 1,800 largest public companies in corporate responsibility and transparency.

In awarding Tyco the 2006 Alexander Hamilton Award in Corporate Governance, *Treasury & Risk* stated, "Tyco has not only rebounded financially—it has become something of a model corporate citizen, with a gleaming new governance ethos, admirable transparency, and an internal ethos that rewards honesty and openness and refuses to tolerate misbehavior or deception. It has been a dramatic turnaround, perhaps unique in recent corporate history in its thoroughness, speed and consistency."[1]

Eric shared the three lessons that have shaped Tyco's governance strategy:

1. Strong functional leadership and mentoring is critical to the ongoing development of high-integrity leaders and employees.
2. Leaders must have a "web of accountability" surrounding them with accountability partners and process disciplines to hold them accountable.
3. Boards and senior management must develop and implement a means to evaluate leadership character.

While a lot of hard work and sheer effort has gone into transforming Tyco's culture, it's also obvious that the right people with
the right mind-set can make a significant difference. Eric shared one
of his favorite quotes. "Billy Graham once stated, 'When a brave
man takes a stand the spines of others are stiffened, '" adding, "All it
takes is just one person who is willing to take a stand for the truth,
then others will follow."

Mentors on a Mission

Eric Pillmore, Randall Zindler, and John Turnipseed each agreed to provide some additional practical advice and inspiration in their area of expertise as "Mentors on a Mission."

Q: Eric, as a leader who's had extensive experience with business cultures, what advice would you give a person who's seeking a culture that aligns with his or her values?

A: Know what you believe. Know what your foundational values are. Ask yourself, What are my non-negotiables? What are the things I absolutely will not compromise? As you research a new job and its environment, find out the answers to these three questions:

❖ What values does this organization stand by?
❖ How does your (future) boss live those values?
❖ How does your boss's boss live those values?

Finally, as you reconcile your non-negotiables with the values of your potential company and the two key individuals above you, ask yourself, What are the obstacles and opportunities of living my values and beliefs?

—Eric Pillmore, Tyco International

Q: Randall, you shared how you felt compelled to leave the comfort and convenience of a business environment to go to a risk-filled and dangerous environment. What advice would you give the reader who wants to make a difference in his or her present environment?

A: For myself and the staff at Medair, our values reflect God's character and ways. We live our values in many troubled spots around the world—Darfur, Uganda, and Congo, to name a few. I certainly would not tell people they need to move to Africa in order to serve God.

We all have our unique calling and passion in life. Each individual has to ask him- or herself, How am I expressing my values at work? Do I get a little involved or really involved? Getting a little involved is a notch up. It's a notch toward getting more involved, if God so desires. The question I would pose to you is, What's the next step up the ladder toward engagement, compassion or leaving one's comfort zone? Could you go one step higher?"

—Randall Zindler, Medair

Q: John, it's inspiring to see how you're impacting an environment that negatively impacted you. What advice would you give the reader who's been negatively impacted by a bad environment yet wants to stay and make a difference?

A: God not only saved me, He took care of me. As I look back on that time period of my life, it's clear to see how God brought people into my life at the right time and place. When I was in prison, Dan Taylor came into my life and encouraged me to get an education. When I was in need of a job, Jane Larson came into my life and offered me my first paying job as a computer-programming teacher. When I was humiliated by the TV news story, Mike Loken provided me with comfort and assurance. Throughout my transformation from gang leader to community leader, Art Erickson, my spiritual mentor, always believed in me and stood by me.

To those people who desire to make a difference in the midst of a bad environment, I would say that God will place good people in your path to help you live and work in a bad environment. Not only will God save you, He will take care of you.

—John Turnipseed, Center for Fathering

Counsel for Consideration

Three leaders. Three environments. Three states of mind. Three points in time. Impact beyond measure—three times over.

And who knows but that you have come to royal position for such a time as this? Perhaps you're like Queen Esther, risking your own life to save another. Perhaps you're similar to Eric Pillmore, actively seizing the moment by seeking out a new environment. Maybe you're like John Turnipseed, changing your current environment over time. Maybe you're fashioned like Randall Zindler, willing to leave the comfort of your job and home to take care of God's beloved children wherever they need you. Or maybe you're uniquely you, being prepared for significant impact and called to be who you are, wherever you are.

Whether your situation calls for waiting and preparation or for immediate action, God has called you for such a time as this. Finding the right place at the right time requires a keen awareness of your environment, state of mind, and the present time. It also takes courage, preparation, and effort.

I believe that being at the right place at the right time is a much simpler proposition than we sometimes make it. A few weeks ago, my wife, Sherri, and I headed to a small hotel for a weekend getaway. We had just completed several months of overwhelming activity—kids' needs, family visits, unplanned home maintenance projects, and a very busy writing schedule.

As we had experienced the prior year, the hotel was not quite what we hoped for and the staff fell somewhat short in their customer-service training. Perhaps that's why they offer a free breakfast. As we sat down to breakfast at a table overlooking the St. Croix River, we were reminded of our previous year's breakfast and the pale, caramel-colored, mildly coffee-flavored water that had accompanied it. Our waitress had explained that management didn't allow her to make the coffee any stronger. Now I don't want to complain—after all, free is free—but when you only get one cup of coffee a day, you want it to be a decent one. Waiting at our table, Sherri and I agreed that we would skip the pseudo-coffee and hold out for a cup at the local coffeehouse.

Bursting onto the scene, a larger-than-life figure approached our table and said, "Hi there, I'm Rhoda! I'm usually the bartender. This morning I'm your waitress." We chatted with Rhoda and found her to be feisty, tough, endearing, full of local flavor, and totally unconventional. In short, she was delightful.

Rhoda took our order and offered us coffee. Declining, Sherri felt she needed to explain. "We understand you aren't allowed to make fully brewed coffee, so we'll just pick some up at Starbucks after breakfast." Rhoda nodded and headed back to the kitchen.

A few minutes later, Rhoda stood before us with a carafe and a whisper. "Here, try this. It's from my private stock. I keep it hidden in the bar." Inside that common-looking carafe was a pot of the darkest, strongest coffee known to mankind. We had entered coffee heaven.

Rhoda was at the right place at the right time. A couple of stressed-out parents in need of a break were the beneficiaries. Minutes—that's all Rhoda spent with us and that's all it took. Sometimes making an impact is as simple as that.

Sometimes things aren't so simple. On August 1, 2007, the world saw the mess of tangled steel and concrete just moments after the tragic collapse of the Minneapolis I-35 bridge into the Mississippi River below. As difficult as it was to know that victims were simply at the wrong place at the wrong time, it was inspiring to hear the stories of everyday heroes who instinctively risked their own lives to save the lives of others. One group of people had no control over their circumstances; the other did. The latter chose to transform an awful circumstance into being at the right place at the right time. Lives were saved through their selfless actions.

I learned three important lessons from that tragedy. First, circumstances have the potential to trigger the best in us. Therefore, we should be motivated to ensure that we're in the environment that brings out our best. Second, the world around us is in a better place when we're in a better place. Having the right state of mind not only benefits us, but also greatly impacts others. Finally, life is short. God instructs us to be ready and walking in the knowledge that we're in a royal position. Our time is right now.

Whether the gift of your place impacts a country, a company, a city, a community, or a couple on a getaway, I believe God has placed you in a royal position for such a time as this.

Prosperity

The Gift of Relationships
as Your Legacy

Issue: What Does It Mean to Live a Prosperous Life?

As director of sales for a large hotel, I was all too familiar with the mantra *Success is a numbers game. The more contacts you have, the greater sales you'll have. The more sales you make, the more money you'll make. The more money you make, the more successful you'll be.* Monthly, I created a "hit list," identifying twenty-five clients and then building strategies and action plans to get sales from these clients. The one constant theme? Getting more from people equals success.

My definition of prosperity was a financial one. The operative words were *getting, accumulating,* and *keeping,* as in getting the sale, accumulating wealth, and keeping stuff. I was like a modern-day caveman, a hunter and a gatherer, except that I hunted with my "hit list" instead of a club and rock. Success afforded me a home, car, furnishings, good wine, and other fun stuff. In times of uncertainty, though, I found myself becoming anxious as I worried about keeping what I had accumulated. I focused more on getting and keeping stuff than on people. Actually, I used people to get stuff.

As I grew in my faith, I began to ask questions and question my goals. Is the greatest reward to be the greatest consumer? Is there an earthly reward greater than financial success? How can I reconcile the world's definition of success with God's definition of success? Is it possible to experience both success and significance in work and life? Bottom line: What does it mean to live a prosperous life?

Solution: Focus on the One to Impact the Many

For what is our hope, our joy, or the crown in which we will glory in the presence of our Lord Jesus when he comes? Is it not you? Indeed, you are our glory and joy.

—1 Thessalonians 2:19–20

The office of my mentor, Monty Sholund, has a wall covered with photographs. They paint quite a picture: family vacations, birth announcements, graduation photos, Christmases, reunions, and business achievements. These are photographs of Monty's students. I think of this as Monty's Prosperity Wall: Lives growing in abundance, maturing spiritually, and reaping fruit in others' lives.

As the ultimate Bible teacher and mentor, Monty's success came by pouring himself into the lives of others so that his students could fulfill their God-given potential. He would ask, "Who would you rather be, Billy Graham or the one who mentored Billy Graham?" His life purpose was to teach and mentor "the one." He believed that if you love the one and encourage and help the one grow in Christ, then the one can impact the world. "Giving yourself to the one equals success," he would say.

While I struggled to write *God Is My CEO*, Monty would remind me, "You aren't writing this book to be a best-seller, you're writing to the one person in need of God's grace." This mental picture of "the one" would help me to focus again. Through God's grace, my books have reached thousands of people worldwide. But I'm just one of the photos on Monty's wall. There are pictures of individuals who have impacted the world in every walk of life. Why? Because Monty focused on the one to impact the many.

Discover the Gift of Relationships as Your Legacy

Elvin Monroe "Monty" Sholund entered the gates of heaven on May 13, 2007, at age eighty-six, during the writing of this book. And those pictures on his wall? The pictures are of people and relationships beloved to Monty. Relationships are Monty Sholund's legacy.

Monty established Village Schools of the Bible in order to teach the Bible in a systematic way and develop students of the Word. He allowed God's Word to pour through him. He drank up the Living Water like a kid on a hot summer day and then poured himself (and God's Word) into others like rain on a parched plant. The world's currency is money, property, and possessions. Monty's currency was people. His joy came from watching others grow in faith, in love, and, ultimately, in their God-given potential.

Just as uncertainty and the unknown are a curse to the one who values possessions, they're a blessing to the one who values people. Uncertainty is a threat to people trying to keep possession of their comfort zones, their money, and their stuff. It creates great anxiety. To the one who values people, however, the unknown is a catalyst for growth.

"We're all going to die," said Rev. Dr. Robert A. Schuller. "The real question is, How are we going to live?" What does it mean to live a prosperous life? To examine this question, we'll first look at the big picture. What is prosperity? God teaches us that eternal significance—God's prosperity—is taking hold of what is truly life. Later in this chapter, we'll study the relationship of mentor to mentee as the conduit of life, the way we become prosperous. Along the way, we'll use Monty's life as an example, to bring glory not to the man, but to the God for whom the man lived.

The Eternal Significance of Taking Hold of That Which Is Truly Life

I used to think that eternal life was something you obtained (through Jesus) at the point of death. I've since discovered that eternal life begins not at physical death, but when we die to ourselves; it begins now! *Eternal* is continuous or never-ending. *Life* is growth and reproduction. *Eternal life* is continuous growth and reproduction. We were created to grow and reproduce, not just physically, but also spiritually. Why wait to take hold of eternal life? Paul urges us in 1 Timothy 6:19 to *take hold of the life that is truly life*.

One of Monty's favorite passages was Galatians 2:20: *I have been crucified with Christ and I no longer live, but Christ lives in me.* By dying to himself, he allowed Christ to live through him. The result was a spark that ignited the spirit in others. The energy and power of the Holy Spirit in him sparked the Holy Spirit within others. Doug Mansfield, one of his students, commented, "Every time I met with Monty I felt like I had been plugged into a high-voltage outlet."

Monty "charged" countless lives that are now charging others. His life and energy are eternal—they continue to grow and flourish worldwide through the relationships he built with others, even though his earthly life has ended. The stories that follow are of four people whose lives Monty impacted. I believe these stories show the prosperity of a life marked by relationships.

Ward Brehm

Ward Brehm is the owner of two Minneapolis-based insurance consulting firms. He explains, "I had the ability to get people from A to Z. I could sell an intangible like life insurance to wealthy people and became very successful at it. I was also very persuasive in the political arena. My wife, who's my best supporter and critic, said, 'Ward, you know what you are? You're a political groupie. You love the glamour of politics. You have access to senators and congressmen and you get to wine and dine in the finest dining rooms in Washington, D.C.'" Ward confessed, "My wife was right. I was so full of myself. Then Monty came along."

Ward's first encounter with Monty occurred shortly after Ward became a Village School student. "I was no doubt among Monty's worst students, if not at the rock bottom. My first paper had *Rubbish!* scrawled across the top. He knew I was capable of better and he would expect nothing less than my best. From that time forward we developed a peculiar friendship at best. We used to have these tremendous arguments. It was uncanny how he knew when to praise and when to push my buttons."

A trip to Africa changed Ward's life. The experience humbled him. "During my walk through Africa, I was amazed to experience the lowest and highest a person can get in this world. I experienced the lowest when I met with the villagers in the jungle. They had the barest of essentials to live on. They lived with no safety net. Then just three days later, I met with President Kagame in the state house in Kigali, Rwanda.

"I came back from Africa with a call of God, but I didn't know what to do. I met with Monty and shared my African experience. I felt guilty living in an affluent suburb, driving my BMW. I asked Monty, 'Should I become a missionary or a teacher?'

"Monty had the gift of exhortation. He had the ability to both encourage and chastise you at the same time. Monty replied, 'If God wanted you to be a missionary, he would have given you patience. If he wanted you to be a teacher, he would have given you intellect.'

"At the same time, he absolutely convinced me that I was going to save Africa. He would enthusiastically implore, 'Your call is Africa!' I would argue, 'How is an insurance salesman going to change Africa?' Monty would shoot back, 'The significance of an event is its future—this is just the beginning!'

"I drew on a piece of paper the highest—the leaders—and the lowest—the destitute. Monty pointed to the poor and exclaimed,

'This is why you're here. Your mission is to help the poor.' Then he pointed to the leaders and said, 'This is your strategy. The best way to help the poor is to change the hearts of the leaders. Use the gifts God has given you. Use your gifts of persuasion that made you successful in convincing the wealthy and powerful and use your political savvy to persuade leaders to help the poor.'

"The mission I'd been seeking was crystallized. I found my sweet spot. Shortly after, Proverbs 31:8 became my life verse: *Speak up for those who cannot speak for themselves, for the rights of all who are destitute.*"

What started as a dream in a small office with the wall covered in photographs became a reality. In May 2004, President George W. Bush appointed Ward Brehm to the board of the United States African Development Foundation. A month later, President Bush named Ward chairman of the foundation. Using relationships built over many years, Ward has been personally involved in peace and reconciliation efforts in Burundi, Rwanda, and the Democratic Republic of Congo, bringing a model of reconciliation based upon faith, friendship, and common understanding. As a voice of the poor, Ward has traveled to Africa thirty times and led teams of American businessmen and members of Congress on trips to Africa.

Ward has been responsible for several significant accomplishments in Africa, but in the end, he's just a humble man passionately fulfilling God's plan. As Ward explains, "I don't fear dying; I fear being irrelevant. Real life is getting involved with something bigger than you."

His passion goes beyond the first step and includes helping another grow so he or she can, in turn, help another. Many of the foundation's investments are in businesses run by women. In 2006, the foundation helped link basket-weaving groups in Tanzania and Ghana to the Target Corporation. This has resulted in sales of hand-woven baskets at Target stores throughout the country and has increased incomes to over 1,100 African women.

Recalling Monty's mentorship, Ward mused, "When the whole world seemed to laugh at your dreams, Monty would embrace them, fuel them with endless prayer, and then relentlessly hold you accountable to the Kingdom for their completion. Monty was the tonic to confusion and a shot in the arm to my discouragement. He always knew that the best way out of any doubt and confusion was to go through it."

Bob "Shoebob" Fisher

"When I think of Monty, two words come up: grace and action. He pounded the message into me, 'Listen and act on what you hear from God.' I was about two-thirds through the Village School course when I came upon Philippians 3:10. The verse stopped me in my tracks. I thought, *Do I really want to know Christ that well?* Monty encouraged me to continue to listen to God and pay attention to what was going on around me."

A few winters later and for no particular reason, Bob decided to do some winter camping. A shoe repairman by day, he purchased a pup tent and pitched it in his backyard. It didn't take long to realize that winter camping in Minnesota had some drawbacks. As the night wore on, Bob started getting cold; so cold that it became very difficult to fall asleep.

As he tossed and turned, trying to keep warm, he recalled the words of Philippians 3:10, *I want to know Christ and the power of his resurrection and the fellowship of sharing in his sufferings, becoming like him in his death.* Then, Bob shares, God spoke to him, saying, "Why don't you move the tent to the front yard and sleep outside to help the needy in Wayzata?"

Bob recalled his perplexed response. "I thought it was a joke! Wayzata is an affluent community where BMWs and Mercedeses are parked along manicured streets. Where were the needy here?"

Through Interfaith Outreach and Community Partners, a local nonprofit organization that provides food, financial assistance, and emergency shelter to those in need, Bob soon discovered that despite Wayzata's affluence, there were still needy people. In November 1996, Bob committed to sleeping in his tent in his front yard until he raised $7,000 to buy Thanksgiving dinners for 100 families. In fourteen days, he raised $10,000.

As Bob learned more about the needy, he realized that the greatest issue was housing. He resolved to repeat his sleepout the following year to help meet the housing needs of families in the community.

One of the most exciting aspects of the Sleep Out is the way it's been embraced by local young people, from kindergartners to college students. The Sleep Out isn't just about helping the homeless, it's about teaching the principles of love, compassion, and service in the hearts of a new generation. "This has become a great way to change an entire generation and a nation as to how to view things," Bob explains. "I show them that one person can make a difference if they would only commit to it and follow through."

Casey, a sixteen-year-old from Minneapolis, wrote to Bob after he spoke at her high school. Her note said, "Hi, I'm Casey Robbins. Well, I used your suggestions and I've been sleeping outside since September 15th and will continue until December 24th. It is 100 nights. . . . So far I have raised about 7,000 dollars which isn't much, but it's a start."

Casey followed with another 100-night sleep out in 2006. Her efforts ignited adults and youth alike to take on the plight of the homeless. When a reporter asked Casey why she's taken on the challenges of the homeless, she responded, "I saw it as something I could do something about."

Over the past eleven years, the Sleep Out has grown from one man's backyard event into a nationwide movement. In addition to raising $8 million for the needy and creating awareness of the real issues of the homeless, Bob has awakened the spirit of Christ's love and compassion in the hearts of others. One shoe repairman's obedience and follow-through to God's still voice has set hearts ablaze in thousands of people who are creating their own sleepouts. From corporations to churches to civic organizations, people are pitching tents and sleeping out, or in some other way volunteering their time and energy.

Anonymous

Following Monty's death, Village Schools received a tribute to him that I found uniquely special. It's evidence that you don't have to change thousands of lives in order to impact the world. You just need to make a difference in one person's life. Here's what the tribute had to say:

> Monty was a man of prayer. Before I even met him, he had been praying for me. Let me back up a bit in order to describe a man who made a profound difference in my life.
>
> In October of 1993, I gave birth to a beautiful, healthy daughter. God's blessing came in spite of the fact that I was unmarried and any relationship I might have had with her father had been mutually severed.
>
> As I moved forward in my life, I desperately cried out to God that my sins would not scar my daughter, that she would know she was loved and that God had a plan for her. My limited human eyes and heart never envisioned or even breathed a prayer that God would involve my daughter's father in the plan He had for the two of us. I just relied on God being enough because I had to and because people were praying. Monty was praying.
>
> Monty, a man unknown to me, knew and loved my daughter's father. They met through Village School and had a long history. Monty had become a mentor to my daughter's father, whose own father had died. Through their relationship, Monty was used to begin the healing in his heart. Monty, always a straightforward encourager, prayed. Monty urged my daughter's father to pray, to pray for her. Eventually, Monty pointed out that prayers for his daughter's well-being necessarily included prayer for her mother, me.

Monty knew the power of prayer. He prayed with faith, believing God's promises. I don't know if Monty ever actually prayed that two wayward adult parents would get back together; I honestly doubt that he did. Nevertheless, I do know that he prayed for God's will in the lives of three people: my daughter, her father, and me.

And just as my prayers were heard, and the prayers of my daughter's father were heard, so were Monty's prayers. God ultimately answered the prayers of my daughter, too. God's timing was seven years. On August 4, 2001, Monty prayed again, this time at a wedding. On that day, my daughter was the flower girl in the wedding of her father and mother.

Without Monty's presence and relationship in the life of my daughter's father, it is unlikely that he and I would be married today. Monty lived a life of prayer and he insisted and persisted in inspiring prayer in others.

Because of the relationship of Monty with one man, a fatherless child now has a two-parent home. Because of prayer, all three in the family believe and pray. Because of Monty's prayerful relationship, a cycle of brokenness ended and a new pattern of living powered by prayer began. That child, our daughter, is a mighty prayer warrior.

From generation to generation, the thread of faith is woven stronger still. Monty's devoted presence in one man's life prospered into the life of a family, living fruit of God's miraculous answer to prayers.

Larry Julian

Years ago Monty told me, "You're not writing this book to be a best-seller; you're writing to the one person in need of God's grace." Still, however, I clung to my definition of success as a numbers game. I'm not sure I really understood how writing to impact one person equated success. A young woman in San Francisco helped change that.

Seven years after my discussion with Monty, my inbox included an e-mail from a young woman who had purchased *God Is My CEO* in China. She shared with me the story of creating a ministry to help the poor in Hunan. She's helping young Chinese girls escape from the trap of slavery and prostitution. The writer thanked me for impacting her life, which in turn has impacted other lives. She closed her e-mail with, "I'm thankful that when you were tempted to not complete the book, you pushed through and did what you knew God wanted you to do."

You never know when your "aha" moment is going to hit you. Her closing sentence helped me understand what Monty had been teaching years ago. Genuine success isn't based on a numbers game or how many books you sell; genuine prosperity comes from reaching the one. Relationships are our legacy.

Monty's words to me so many years ago when I wanted to quit writing—"Larry, I think the book has become your idol. Perhaps God is testing and humbling you to see what's really in your heart"—had convicted me to the core. After much prayer, I made the decision to continue my quest to find a publisher for *God Is My CEO.*

As I look back on the continuous nature of one's eternal life, I see how God worked through Monty to help me discover this all-surpassing power. Discovering it and persevering helped one woman in Hunan, China. One woman, in turn, has created a ministry to help save at least one young Chinese girl from prostitution.

While Monty is busy with all the saints who've gone before him, the Holy Spirit that lived in him has been passed on to others, and his legacy continues to live and grow. Perhaps Casey, the young girl inspired by Bob Fisher's Sleep Out, will take the mantle and inspire a new generation of youth to help the homeless. Perhaps a young Chinese girl who's been saved from slavery will go on to ignite freedom throughout China. Perhaps the daughter who saw her parents united through the power of prayer will impact a nation through her prayers. Focusing on the one impacts the many.

Mentor on a Mission

I visited Monty in the hospital about a week before he passed away. As he slipped in and out of consciousness, my expectation was just to be with him. His labored breathing now made it difficult for him to speak, so I said, "Monty, don't try to talk; just relax." I knew he enjoyed listening to reports of his students' activity and growth, so I began to fill the silence with an update on the writing of *God Is My Coach*.

Suddenly, Monty's nearly lifeless body rose to attention, his distant eyes came into focus, and he looked intently into my eyes. With a clear and authoritative voice, Monty rattled off one of his favorite teaching points, proclaiming, "There are five E's to Effective Mentorship: Encounter, Engage, Enlighten, Encourage, and Enjoy."

Monty proceeded to teach this appreciative student with the power of the Holy Spirit. I found it prophetic that a man so close to physical death was so spiritually alive; the living embodiment of the words of 2 Corinthians 4:11–12: *For we who are alive are always being given over to death for Jesus' sake, so that his life may be revealed in our mortal body. So then, death is at work in us, but life is at work in you.*

How fitting and profound it is that the final "Mentor on a Mission" is Monty Sholund, teacher and founder of Village Schools of the Bible. Since his great voice is now heard only in heaven, the Five E's of Effective Mentorship will be shared through the stories of some of the people Monty has mentored. I pray that you are able to use this practical tool to ignite this all-surpassing power that is at work in you.

The Five E's of Effective Mentorship

1. Encounter: Discern Hidden Potential in the Hearts of Others

To encounter is to come upon face-to-face, perhaps as a chance meeting with a stranger or a get-together with an individual with whom you have a relationship. Monty was always interested in others' lives. As his former secretary, Barb Gretch, observed, "I saw him pour himself into the lives of others. I saw him share the love of the Lord with the postman, the copier repairman, the pizza delivery guy. It was just a natural outflow of who he was. Personally, I never saw Monty as 'having a ministry.' Monty's work was indistinguishable from who he was."

A mentor has a keen alertness of a person's potential. A mentor is also discerning in terms of how best to pursue a relationship. Monty was very intentional. He not only saw the potential in people, he sought out the ones who had a passion to pursue God's potential in themselves. As a leader and mentor, you cannot give yourself to all people. You would burn yourself out and render yourself ineffective. Jesus encountered thousands of people but chose only twelve disciples. He was intentional about his choices; he didn't choose the twelve by talent or position, but sought out hearts that had passion and potential waiting to be ignited.

2. Engage: With Love and Truth, Unleash the Potential in Another

Engagement has two definitions. One is to bind or join together, such as a man and woman who make a pledge to one another. The second is to enter into battle, as in engaging the enemy. Both definitions are important.

Love and truth are the two elements of engagement. Love binds the mentor and mentee; there is a mutual love and respect for one another. One person desires to teach and the other desires to learn. Where love binds, truth confronts and challenges. An effective mentor reveals truth that a mentee either doesn't recognize or doesn't want to hear. The mentor battles the obstacles that keep the mentee from seeing the truth.

Love and truth must be combined to be effective. Truth without love can be harsh, condescending, and judgmental. 1 Corinthians 13:2–3 reminds us, *If I have a faith that can move mountains, but have not love, I am nothing. If I give all I possess to the poor and surrender my body to the flames, but have not love, I gain nothing.* Alternatively, love without truth may provide comfort, but limits the mentee's ability to learn and grow.

Truth and love together create a powerful life force. Love affirms the dignity of the individual and the truth helps the individual grow. Monty wielded truth and love like a skilled surgeon in an operating room. He knew that confronting the truth might hurt but also knew it could heal. Where the truth challenges, convicts, and confronts, love always connects, waits, protects, and hopes.

One of Monty's students, Widdy Bird, enthusiastically recalled their initial engagement. "Monty and I had a rough start. Long before I was a Christian, I somehow landed in one of Monty's classes. About the third class, Monty hit all of my politically correct, feminist hot buttons. I marched up to Monty after class, shaking my finger at him. 'Just who do you think you are, saying God will condemn those people! You're so judgmental! Our God is better than that, Monty!' Monty didn't flinch. He moved a little closer to me and asked, 'Just how much do you know about our God, anyway?' Completely insulted, I turned on my heels and marched out of the room, slamming the door behind me, swearing I'd never come back. But I did come back, five years later, to take Monty's course again. Halfway through the course, I had fallen head over heels in love with God."

In business today, leadership coaching has become a hot commodity. While it can be effective, it often falls short of its potential. In an attempt not to offend, a coach or mentor may share what the student wants to hear and not what he needs to hear. A Jewish proverb states, "Better the ugly truth than a beautiful lie." Monty never compromised the truth. Because he loved God and others, anything less would be a disservice to both.

Three hundred former students, mentees, and friends came to Monty's memorial service. After hearing the remarks of those who eulogized Monty earlier in the service, Chris Conger, a beloved student of Monty's, exclaimed, "I thought I was the only one Monty loved until I came here!" Monty made you feel as if you were the most important person on earth.

High levels of disengagement are the norm in business and family relationships today. In fact, sharing truth may seem more of a detriment than a benefit. Imagine, though, receiving the total attention and love of someone you respect. Now imagine that same individual setting standards of excellence and challenging you to fulfill your God-given potential while loving you as you are, with all your faults and failures. Love and truth together make up a powerful force for engaging another. In the end, love doesn't teach the truth; love reveals the truth.

3. Enlighten: Help Another Find His or Her Call

To enlighten is to give spiritual insight into something that isn't readily evident. Our calling and direction in life, for example, is a truth most of us search for but don't find readily evident. Our calling is often buried under the busyness and distractions of our daily lives. Fears, doubts, pressures, and insecurities dim the spirit of God that lies within us. An effective mentor acts as a guide to help another find his or her way through confusion in order to find clarity and direction.

If one's calling is a circuit breaker, then the mentor's role is to get the flashlight, use the flashlight to guide the mentee to the circuit breaker, and then shed light on the switch. The mentee is responsible for flipping the switch and turning the power on.

Remember the conversation between Monty and Ward Brehm when Ward returned from Africa? Ward knew God had stirred his heart for Africa but he didn't know what to do with that hidden stirring. Monty enlightened Ward by providing a deeper spiritual insight; one Ward couldn't see. He helped bring clarity and direction when he pointed to the poor and said "That's your mission" and pointed to the powerful and said "That's your strategy." The switch within Ward's heart flipped.

Ephesians 1:17–19 says, *I keep asking that the God of our Lord Jesus Christ, the glorious Father, may give you the Spirit of wisdom and revelation, so that you may know him better. I pray also that the eyes of your heart may be enlightened in order that you may know the hope to which he has called you, the riches of his glorious inheritance in the saints, and his incomparably great power for us who believe.* Thus is the role of the mentor, to help his or her student to know God better. As Monty understood, enlightenment not only reveals God's call, but also provides the hidden rewards and the power to follow through on the call.

4. Encourage: Believe in Others When They Don't Believe in Themselves

To encourage is to inspire with courage, spirit, and hope. It implies breathing life, energy, and confidence into another. Encouragement by Monty changed Chris Conger's life.

"I met Monty during a Village School Saturday School," Chris began. "At the time, I was directionless with no purpose or plan for my life. I was a thirty-two-year-old working on a factory line by day and a jock weightlifter in my free time. I was intrigued by Monty's class but intimidated about writing papers. One night after class, I worked up courage and followed Monty out to his car. I asked, 'Will you disciple me?' I had no idea how much my life would change.

"Monty believed in me. I had very low self-esteem, so I couldn't ever understand why he believed in me. I remember him saying, 'Chris, you need to learn to love yourself as a child of God redeemed. You can't believe in yourself until you love yourself.'

"After a while, I asked Monty about my future. 'You should go to college,' he responded. I thought, *I can't do that—I barely graduated high school!* Monty taught me a simple prayer: 'God, give me a hunger for your Word that I do not possess but a hunger that possesses me.' I prayed that prayer for years on my way to work every morning. My most rewarding moment was when I called Monty and said, 'I'm going to college!' When I found it intimidating, I would call Monty and he would say, 'Relax, give your human best filled with the Holy Spirit and leave the rest to God.' I was the first person in my family of ten to receive a four-year college degree. I graduated from Oak Hills Bible College with honors."

Today, Chris is the senior pastor at White Oak Bible Chapel in Brainerd, Minnesota. He explained what his purpose and direction is now: "By grace, my life can encourage someone else's life the way Monty's life, by grace, encouraged me. It isn't what I can do for God, it's what God by grace can and will do through me for His glory." A person who once lacked direction and confidence now lives a bold life of purpose.

A mentor goes beyond enlightening people regarding their call to encourage them to pursue it. Even the most confident leader has bouts of doubt. Doug Mansfield, one of Monty's mentees, explained, "For some reason, Monty seemed to think I had something to offer the world. I was completely stunned that he thought my ideas were worth anything. I felt so utterly stupid." Another of Monty's students summed up the meaning of encouragement: "When I went to talk to Monty about impossibilities, he always saw possibilities. He would say, 'It doesn't matter what happens, it only matters what happens to what happens.'"

5. Enjoy: Experience the Joy of Seeing Others Grow

Until now, we've talked about the rewards and rationale of giving over getting. Our final E, to enjoy, means to *take* pleasure or satisfaction in giving to something or someone.

Monty was my mentor for thirteen years. I confess that our relationship was somewhat lopsided; I got the better end of the deal. Monty taught me, comforted me, encouraged me, and helped me. Looking back, however, I see a pattern. Monty demonstrated true joy over our relationship. At first, I thought it was a ploy to give me confidence. Over time, I came to understand that he actually felt true joy. He was *overjoyed* when *God Is My CEO* was finally published. He was excited to hear about my business ventures and the role I was taking to help people integrate their work and faith. Every life event, from my marriage to the births of our children, brought him joy. Monty absolutely loved to see a student find his or her call and fulfill his or her potential.

It was only recently that I began to consider myself a mentor. Not a coach, but a mentor, one who is seriously committed to helping another fulfill his potential. One of Monty's great truths, known to every Village School student, is "What you share you keep." Until I began to mentor, I had difficulty grasping the meaning of that concept. I can tell you that I've learned more and experienced more satisfaction in a brief time as a mentor than in all my years as a mentee. A recovering self-help junkie, I've discovered the value in enriching another's life. By mentoring, I have the ability to play a small yet significant role in God's greater plan.

Counsel for Consideration

Richard Dawkins, an atheist who wrote *The God Delusion,* was asked, "What would you most like to tell people of faith?" He responded, "Be skeptical—truly examine your faith. Ask yourself if there is any evidence for your beliefs."

As I gathered the evidence of Monty's life in as unbiased a manner as possible, I found myself going down two distinct tracks. First, I found myself falling into the trap of success equals numbers. As I began to count all the lives impacted by Monty's life, I was overwhelmed. I wanted to pick up the phone, call Mr. Dawkins, and exclaim, "Look at this *great man* of faith! Look at the lives one man has impacted all over the world!"

Then I calmed down and discovered the other perspective. "Mr. Dawkins," I would say, "look at this man of *great faith*. Just look at how Monty Sholund reflected Jesus and impacted the one in need of God's grace." It wasn't so much that Monty was a great man but that he allowed us to see a great God.

Charles Yue, a student of Monty's who now disciples others, recently said, "In life, there are role models and there are heroes. Role models are emulated for what they do well, while heroes are admired for who they are. Monty was more than a role model to me; he was a hero. Like everyone else, he had doubts, fears, and discouragements, but he never allowed them to be relevant in the purpose God had for his life—to be like His Son. Instead, I experienced an unmistakable freedom and joy in the man; I caught a glimpse of the character of the heart and spirit of Jesus—*the pearl* (Matthew 13:46). I didn't seek to emulate what Monty had accomplished, but what he found that gave him the freedom and joy to become who he was. I want that pearl!"

A letter from Lorraine Allenbach expressed the thoughts of many. She wrote: "When Monty went home to Jesus, and I started reading the testimonies about him, I wondered how my own life would reflect Jesus when the time came to say 'so long.' Would anyone have found encouragement and light for the Journey because of my life? Would folks, with tears in their eyes and joy in their hearts, say, 'Well done, good and faithful servant of the Lord'? Did I always have an encouraging word, a glow of peace from within, a Scripture-based word to guide and uplift a wandering or sorrowing brother? Would anyone be inspired to greater love, obedience and service to Jesus because of my life and testimony? For all these things, I thank the Lord for Monty, because he showed so many of us the way of love, obedience, joy, perseverance, servanthood, and devotion. His life was a beacon showing the way to Jesus—I want my life to be like that too!"

My Closing Thoughts

Monty was a great man of faith and a man of great faith. He would be appalled, however, if he thought someone wanted to emulate him. Why? Because God has specifically created each of us with a unique purpose, giftedness, and plan. Monty has already fulfilled God's plan for his life. Now it's our turn to fulfill God's plan for our lives.

Yes, we each want that pearl. We desire love, joy, and peace in our lives and in the lives of those we touch. We desire to serve a greater purpose and live a life of significance. We want to be a beacon of light that touches others.

When you clear a path for God to be significant in your life, you create a path for God to be significant in other people's lives. That's why *your* life is so important. You don't need to change the world and do great things for God. Let God help you be a good husband, wife, parent, friend, leader, or co-worker. The world is starved for the pearl that is within *you*!

Your life as an expression of your faith, even with your blemishes and faults, has an impact on the world around you. Don't allow your blemishes to diminish God's blessings. Expose them as an expression of your faith. Ephesians 2:10 says, *For we are God's workmanship, created in Christ Jesus to do good works, which God prepared in advance for us to do.* You may see a flawed person; God sees a masterpiece. Within you lies the power and magnificence of a Holy God.

Finally, let's take a moment to think about God's message in John 15:16: *You did not choose me, but I chose you and appointed you to go and bear fruit—fruit that will last.* God has uniquely created, gifted, and chosen you to go and bear fruit. When Paul urged us to *take hold of life that is truly life,* he was urging us to take hold of an eternal life—one that begins now.

Perhaps you're thinking, *This is too great a task; this is too hard to do.* In response, Monty would tell you, "Relax! Pursue your loving relationship with God and out of you will flow rivers of living water. The fountain is doing what comes naturally and spontaneously, constantly delivering refreshment to the thirsty."

A life that uniquely experiences and reflects God's power isn't fulfilling a command or a duty; it does so out of privilege and honor. It's not a life of straining to produce numbers in order to prove worth, but a life that naturally flows with an endless supply that refreshes the one in need of refreshment. This is the fruit that is within your grasp now and for eternity.

What does it mean to live a prosperous life? We prosper when relationships are our legacy (1 Thessalonians 2:19–20). As Barb Gretch recalled, "Monty had a special way of teaching about the 'crown of rejoicing.' He shared that someday the assembled saints of all the ages will gather before the King of Glory to worship Him and the crowns that we will lay at His feet will be the people whom God has reached through us. I will be a crown that Monty will present to the Lord."

What an incredible day that will be. As you continue on this eternal life, I wish for you a future filled with prosperity, one that overflows with a legacy of relationships.

We began this journey so many pages ago facing chaos and un-certainty, yet knowing that our true greatness as leaders lies within the gray. I hope that living with the questions of your uncertainty has opened your heart to new truths, and that the truth revealed has unraveled some of the uncertainties of your situation. I hope you have a clearer understanding of yourself and greater confidence in your decisions and direction. I hope you better understand the eternal significance of your uncertainty; most especially that your uncertainty is an instrument for God's noble purpose.

And, of course, I genuinely hope you've discovered the blessing of each of the gifts in the gray: Your purpose, your potential, your perspective, your platform, your power, your pace, your place, and your prosperity. Through them, may you receive gifts in the gray and clarity in your uncertainty.

GOD IS MY COACH LIFE PLAN

This special section includes exercises to help you identify and develop each of the eight gifts. More importantly, this section is practical—this is where you understand how the gifts of uncertainty apply to *you*. As each of the gifts in the gray is revealed to you, document your discoveries in the "My Life Plan Summary" chart on the last page of this section.

Purpose: The Gift of Your Unique Calling

Discovering Your Unique Giftedness

God has been leaving you clues about your giftedness your entire life; now it's time to discover them. We've learned that there are five areas that make up your unique giftedness. These five areas of giftedness are buried within the stories of your past and present.

In this exercise, you'll document three brief stories and then, as if on a treasure hunt, you'll look for the five themes of your unique giftedness. As you piece these themes together, you'll begin to see the weavings of a beautiful tapestry. The tapestry will reveal your unique giftedness. Let's walk through the process.

Step one: Identify the moments that have brought you the most joy and satisfaction.

With paper in hand, identify the three most satisfying achievements of your life. Write a brief story about each one. If possible, choose one story from childhood, one from young adulthood, and one from your adult and/or career years. Each story needs to fulfill these three criteria: you enjoyed doing it, you did it well, and you accomplished something that brought you personal satisfaction.

Step two: Write a brief description for each of your stories.

In one or two paragraphs, describe the details of what you did to achieve those satisfying moments. Document the actions and activities you were involved in. For example, "As a corporate trainee, I organized the company picnic. I started by creating a plan with two co-workers, then I enlisted the help of other managers. I sold more Girl Scout cookies than anyone else. . . ."

Step three: For each story, answer five questions.

Each question represents one of the five themes that comprise your giftedness. Identify your recurring themes by prayerfully answering each of the five questions for each of your three stories (as in the previous steps, record your answers).

1. Abilities: What did you do that you enjoyed? (Hint: Identify the verbs in each story, such as *organized, created, enlisted,* etc.)
2. Subject matter: What kind of things, ideas, and/or people were you working with?
3. Circumstances: What kind of environment or circumstances were present?
4. Operating relationships: What role or roles did you play?
5. Payoff: What was the payoff? What was the most rewarding or satisfying aspect of your story?

Step four: Weave in the five recurring themes to create a picture of your unique giftedness.

Complete the following table with the responses from your stories.

Abilities My natural strengths and abilities are . . .	**Abilities**
Subject Matter The things I love to work with most are . . .	**Subject Matter**
Circumstances I'm most alive when I work under these conditions or environments . . .	**Circumstances**
Operating Relationships I'm most effective when I'm in the role of . . .	**Operating Relationships**
Payoff I'm most satisfied and feel the most joy from my achievement when . . .	**Payoff**

Are you beginning to discover how you've been gifted? I urge you to dwell on these five components. Understanding them will help direct your energies to those choices which best match your unique giftedness. For further research on this subject, I encourage you to visit the "Other Resources" section of this book.

Potential: The Gift of Creativity

Unlocking Your Creative Potential: Open Your I's

Art Erickson's creativity was spurred on with questions like *How do we reach the unreached? How can we impact fathers so they can impact their kids?* The best way to "Open Your I's" is to begin with questions. Meditate on and answer these questions, then record your responses.

1. *Invest: Take an honest look at your God-given resources.*
   ❖ How are you presently investing your time, talents, and resources?
   ❖ What are you willing to risk and even sacrifice in order to fulfill your potential?

2. *Investigate: Where is God working?*
   ❖ What people tend to grab your attention the most?
   ❖ What is their pain?
   ❖ What issue or problem do you see?
   ❖ What unmet need do you see?
   ❖ What stirs your heart?

3. *Illuminate: Create an insight journal to capture your insights, ideas, and thoughts.*
   ❖ What are your insights, ideas, and thoughts telling you?

4. *Imagine: Allow yourself to daydream and imagine a vision greater than yourself, then free your mind to think about the improbable, impractical, and impossible.*

❖ How will your target market (those you identified in the Investigate stage) benefit from your vision?

❖ What insights and ideas can you take from the Illuminate stage to transform into baby steps or programs that align with your vision?

5. *Incubate: Dwell on your ideas in order to birth your vision.*

❖ What ideas need to be nurtured in order to grow?

❖ What ideas need to be put on the shelf for now?

❖ How do you need to grow in order to give birth to the idea?

6. *Innovate: Transform your ideas into a practical plan.*

❖ What tangible product or service are you marketing?

❖ How do these products and services specifically fulfill the needs of your target market?

❖ How will you bring these products and services to the marketplace?

7. *Improvise: Build flexibility and adaptability into your plan.*

❖ Are you willing to share your ideas with others or even let go of them?

❖ How do you respond to problems, obstacles, and rejection?

❖ Are you comfortable knowing your ideas and plans may morph into an unexpected new direction?

Once you've answered each question, step back and look at the seven I's as a whole. As succinctly as possible, describe your peanut.

Perspective: The Gift of Appreciation

Express Your Thanks to God

In this exercise, you'll write a thank-you letter to God. First, take some time to discern His hidden blessings. This includes those intangible things that aren't easily seen, such as positive memories, a talent for art, the joy of watching sunsets, etc. Next, on a blank piece of paper, list what you have. This includes tangible items such as a loving wife, good health, a home, and so on.

Now, consolidate your blessings into the three blessings you appreciate the most. Conclude your letter with a brief but pure expression of thanks to God.

Express Your Thanks to Another

Identify three people in your life to whom you would like to creatively express your appreciation. Consider those you work with, your family members, and people from your past. In the fashion most comfortable to you (i.e., in person, through e-mail, card, or letter, or through some other act of love), communicate a sincere expression of your gratitude.

Here are some criteria to consider:

❖ Be sincere (from the heart and genuine)
❖ Be specific (specifically identify how this person positively impacted you)
❖ Be selfless (expect nothing in return)
❖ Be significant (your thanks, encouragement, and inspiration will be of value and importance to the recipient)

Platform: The Gift of Your Foundation

Building Your Platform

Picture yourself building a platform on which you'll communicate who you are to the world. Since your platform needs to be solid, you'll place four cornerstones, one securely in each corner. Your platform, or communication, can be only as effective as the strength of the cornerstones that support it.

Perspective A: Through Your Eyes

Take an honest look at your actions and behaviors and answer the following questions:

Cornerstone 1: Reconcile
How do you reconcile your beliefs (who you are) with your communication (actions, decisions, behaviors, and written and verbal communications)?

Cornerstone 2: Respect
How do you show respect to others at work and at home?

Cornerstone 3: Reflect
How do you reflect the love, nature, and character of God at work and at home?

Cornerstone 4: Raise
How do you raise the standards of excellence and quality of life at work and at home?

Perspective B: Through Others' Eyes

Choose two or three people who love you and who will be honest with you. Ideally, you would choose one member of your family and one or two people from your work setting. Have them answer the following questions and return their responses to you.

Cornerstone 1: Reconcile
Do [your name]'s actions, decisions, behavior, and communication reflect his/her beliefs?

Cornerstone 2: Respect
Does [your name] show you respect? Please respond and explain your answer, providing examples to [your name] to be used as constructive feedback.

Cornerstone 3: Reflect
In what ways does [your name] reflect the love, nature, and character of God?

Cornerstone 4: Raise
How does [your name] improve the quality of life for you and those around you?

After you've completed your self-evaluation and received feedback from loved ones and co-workers, review the integrity of your foundation. Is it solid or are there some cracks in your foundation? If you discovered flaws in your platform, what steps can you take to solidify your foundation?

Power: The Gift of Pressure
The four exercises of this practical application will walk you through the steps to transforming pressure into power and allow you to apply it to your own situation.

Awareness: Seeing your circumstances from God's perspective.
1. Conduct a scan of your present circumstances:
   a. What positive pressure do you feel, such as a calling, leadership opportunity, etc.?
   b. What negative stress is burdening you, such as concern about a financial goal, being angered by a boss or co-worker, etc.?
2. Using the gifts of wisdom and discernment, what are your internal thoughts and external circumstances communicating to you?

Alignment: Transforming negative tendencies into creative tension.
1. Review The Highway of Life Chart:
   a. Which shoulder most reflects your tendencies under pressure? Do you tend to neglect your gifts or abuse your gifts?
   b. What are your specific habits and tendencies under pressure?
2. Identify a negative stress you are presently experiencing. Turn this pressure into a specific question for God. (For example, I'm feeling overwhelmed by a project. The pressure is causing me to fight with a co-worker who's not pulling his weight and causing delays. How can I be a good team leader and get this project done on time?)
3. Have a prayerful creative tension dialogue with God. Write down the thoughts and insights that are generated from this time.

Adaptability: Develop resiliency in uncertainty.
1. From your creative tension dialogue with God, identify the thoughts, behaviors, and actions you should consider modifying.

2. What thought or behavior are you willing to surrender to God?

Action: Wisdom plus action equals obedience.

1. Which do you believe is the most appropriate response to your situation?
   a. I have all the wisdom needed, it's time to act; or
   b. I need more wisdom before taking action.
2. What next step is required to move closer toward your power zone?

Pace: The Gift of Grace to Run Your Race

What's Your Pace?

In this exercise, we'll examine two different times in your life. First, think about a time period or situation when you felt you were "off your pace," or moving too fast or too slow for your comfort level. What was taking you off your pace? Was it a boss? A situation? A wrong attitude or belief? Try to specifically identify what caused you to operate outside of your natural rhythm.

Now think about and describe a time when you were in your natural rhythm. What was it about that time period or situation that gave you strength and energy?

Based on the insights from these two experiences, what do you think God is telling you about your natural pace? How can you apply this insight to recalibrate your present pace?

What's Your Race?

Take a few minutes to think about and meditate on the race you're in—both personally and professionally. Does the quiet, still voice of God tell you that you're running the race He's uniquely marked out for you? Do you feel He's telling you that you may be running someone else's race? Regardless of your response, pray for direction, clarity, and guidance regarding your next step.

If you feel you're not running the race God marked out for you, is God telling you to persevere in your current race because He's still preparing you for the next race? Is He telling you it's time to take a leap of faith and find your unique race? I urge you to seek God's direction on this important issue.

Place: The Gift of Your Environment

The Right Place at the Right Time

Identify a time in your life when you felt like you were in the right place at the right time.

- ❖ Describe the environment and/or circumstances.
- ❖ Describe your state of mind.
- ❖ Describe the timing.

We can never fully know the significance of a particular place in time, nor can we measure the impact our actions have had on others. With that said, what do you *think* was the impact and significance of your right place at the right time experience?

How can you use that experience to guide you as you discern which future cultures and environments are best for you?

Prosperity: The Gift of Relationships as Your Legacy

Defining Prosperity

With a blank sheet of paper or journal page in front of you, take some time to meditate on your definition of *prosperity*. When you're ready, record your definition.

Then, with God's guidance, think about how you're going to

go about it. In other words, using your unique purpose, potential, platform, pace, and place, determine what kind of relationships will be your legacy and how you will initiate and/or enhance those relationships.

Document your plan and identify what, if any, additional resources (i.e., further Bible study, research on a particular topic, etc.) you need to put your plan into action.

Be a Hero to Someone

One of the best ways to find clarity and direction in the midst of uncertainty is to focus your attention on another, rather than on yourself. The goal of this exercise is to be a hero to someone simply by being you. Often, the greatest gift you can give another isn't money, advice, or expertise; it's you. Investing in one person's potential can change the world for generations to come. In this exercise, you'll identify the person whom God desires you to mentor.

Use the Five E's to Effective Mentorship as your general guide. In this exercise, we'll focus only on the first E: encounter. The goal of encounter is to seek out someone to mentor.

Mentoring is traditionally considered part of a professional relationship, i.e., helping a novice in your field of expertise. For this exercise, however, I encourage you to expand your insights beyond your business relationships to include people in all aspects of your life. Consider your son, daughter, co-worker, an at-risk youth, a neighbor, etc. Prayerfully, ask God to reveal to you the *one person* who is in need of His love, grace, and truth. Then, with patience and wisdom, discern the right mentoring relationship.

Document your thoughts on the mentoring relationship and determine how and when you'll begin. Review the remaining E's: engage, enlighten, encourage, and then enjoy the experience of seeing another grow!

My Life Plan Summary

Eight Questions	Eight Gifts	My Discoveries
Chapter 1: Purpose How can I integrate my career with my calling?	The Gift of My Unique Calling	
Chapter 2: Potential How can I fulfill my God-given potential?	The Gift of Creativity	
Chapter 3: Perspective How can I avoid becoming mired in my circumstances?	The Gift of Appreciation	
Chapter 4: Platform How do I live and communicate my faith in a diverse environment?	The Gift of My Foundation	
Chapter 5: Power How can I keep pressure from getting the best of me?	The Gift of Pressure	
Chapter 6: Pace How can I keep from being overwhelmed by urgent work demands?	The Gift of Grace to Run My Race	
Chapter 7: Place What's the best work environment for me?	The Gift of My Environment	
Chapter 8: Prosperity What does it mean to live a prosperous life?	The Gift of Relationships as My Legacy	

GOD IS MY COACH DISCUSSION GUIDE

Open and honest discussion on applying faith to real-life issues is an important part of your growth and development. The questions in this section will help guide your meetings and connect you with your trusted associates.

Purpose: The Gift of Your Unique Calling

1. Describe how you use your unique giftedness at work. Give examples.
2. What are the obstacles to fully utilizing your gifts at work? Explain.
3. What clues toward your calling have you discovered in your giftedness?
4. How do you reconcile your career with your calling?
5. Describe your ideal job (the one that uses your "sweet spot," which is when you're doing what you love and do well).
6. What small steps could you take toward making your ideal job a reality?
7. What was your biggest revelation from the "Discovering Your Unique Giftedness" exercise?

Potential: The Gift of Creativity

This chapter's discussion will have a different design than the other chapters. Prior to the discussion group meeting, complete the "Unlocking Your Creative Potential" exercise from the "God Is My Coach Life Plan" section on pages 174–175. Using your responses to the questions in this exercise, you can design your discussion group in one of two ways:

Design 1

Pair members into partners. Allowing up to ten minutes for each "I" (five minutes per partner), one partner will provide their answers while the other partner listens and responds. Then switch roles.

Design 2

Allow each member the opportunity to present their responses while the other members take on the role of an advisory board. Each person will take a turn to describe their entire peanut (responses to the seven I's). The remaining participants act as an informal advisory board giving the appropriate feedback. Determine in advance how much time will be dedicated to each individual based on the length of your meeting and the number of members who wish to present their "peanut."

Perspective: The Gift of Appreciation

1. In what ways do your circumstances negatively impact your perspective?
2. Give an example of how trusting in the unseen helped you through a challenging circumstance.
3. What gifts has God given that you tend to take for granted?
4. How can you transform the gifts you take for granted into opportunities to express appreciation?
5. How do you view your family? Your work? Your life?
6. How can you express your appreciation to God in each of these areas?
7. Think about Fred Harburg's advice in "Mentor on a Mission." Identify and discuss a practical step you can take to apply appreciation in your work setting.

Platform: The Gift of Your Foundation

1. What issues and obstacles hinder your ability to live and communicate your faith at work?
2. To date, how have you handled this sensitive issue?
3. Is sharing one's faith appropriate for today's workplace? Please explain your opinion.
4. What have been the implications (good or bad) of exposing your faith at work? As a group, identify on a flip chart the good and bad outcomes of sharing one's faith at work.
5. Does defining who you are help or hinder your leadership effectiveness at work? As a group, identify on a flip chart how your platform can improve or hinder your leadership effectiveness.
6. What's a concrete way you can show respect to others at work? At home?
7. What's the most important insight you'll take away from this chapter?

Power: The Gift of Pressure

1. Under what circumstances are you most energized at work? What triggers your energy?
2. Under what circumstances are you least energized at work? What causes your energy to drain?
3. How do you balance work and rest to keep your energy up during the day?
4. Describe a "sweet spot" moment when you've utilized your gifts under pressure in your power zone.
5. How do you transform pressure into power?

Pace: The Gift of Grace to Run Your Race

1. What do you believe is the race God marked out for you?

2. Are you running your race or someone else's race? Please explain.

3. What is your natural pace? Do you tend to be a turtle or a hare? Describe your God-given pace.

4. When do you find it difficult to run at your God-given pace?

5. What does it mean to do your best?

6. How do you know when you've given your best?

7. Complete this sentence: In order to run with perseverance the race marked out for me, I will _____ _____.

Place: The Gift of Your Environment

1. Describe your present work environment.

2. Does your present environment help or hinder your motivation and inspiration?

3. What elements of your environment (i.e., problems, opportunities, people you work with, needs of others, etc.) fuel your motivations?

4. Do you feel your situation calls for waiting and preparation or for immediate action? Please explain.

5. What do you need to change to help you be in the right place at the right time? Please describe.
   - ❖ Your environment?
   - ❖ Your state of mind?
   - ❖ The timing?

Prosperity: The Gift of Relationships as Your Legacy

1. How do you define prosperity?

2. Think about someone who mentored you in some way. What was it about that individual that impacted you?

3. Have you ever mentored an individual? If so, share how you've benefited from the relationship.

4. What do you think about the concept of focusing on the one to impact the many? Do you agree or disagree that giving yourself to the one equals success?

5. Share your insights from the "Five E's of Effective Mentorship" exercise with another.

   ❖ In what areas do you need to grow in order to be a more effective member?

   ❖ How can you help each other fulfill this assignment?

ADDITIONAL RESOURCES BY LARRY JULIAN

God Is My CEO: Following God's Principles in a Bottom-Line World, published by Adams Media Corporation (2001)

Many leaders struggle with the dilemma of being successful and living a life with purpose. Often, their personal beliefs seem to conflict with the bottom-line demands of today's business world. *God Is My CEO* offers a practical and inspirational source of guidance for integrating one's work and faith.

"Surely for the faithful, Julian's book must arrive as a comfort in corporate times, a balm in business, a printed sanctuary for souls strained in the modern workplace."

—CNN.com

"Larry Julian's *God Is My CEO* is a serious work, capturing some of the difficulty of combining Christianity and capitalism."

—*The Wall Street Journal*

To learn more about Larry's books and other resources, visit www.larryjulian.com.

God Is My Success: Transforming Adversity into Your Destiny, published by Warner Faith (2005)

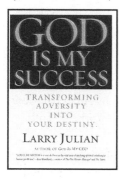

God Is My Success shows that your adversity holds the key to your destiny and the success God intended. As we partner with God to overcome our obstacles, we discover that, ultimately, God Himself is our success. From pain, discover destiny. From financial slavery, discover financial freedom. From lack of confidence, discover courage. From distractions, discover God's whisper. From fear and worry, discover peace.

"*God Is My Success* is a tour de force in the vital area of applying spiritual solutions to human problems."
—Ken Blanchard, co-author of
The One Minute Manager and *The Secret*

To learn more about Larry's books and other resources, visit www.larryjulian.com.

OTHER RESOURCES

Purpose: The Gift of Your Unique Calling

To learn more about Rosalind Cook and her art, visit www.rosalindcook.com.

To discover more about People Management International, visit www.peoplemanagement.org.

Arthur F. Miller, Jr. with William Hendricks, *The Power of Uniqueness: How to Become Who You Really Are,* Zondervan (1999).

Max Lucado, *Cure for the Common Life: Living in Your Sweet Spot,* W Publishing Group (2005).

Potential: The Gift of Creativity

To find out more about Urban Ventures, visit www.urbanventures.org.

Perspective: The Gift of Appreciation

To discover more about Go Latino!, visit www.GoLatino.org or www.urbanventures.org. To contact Susana Espinosa de Sygulla, visit www.sourceofjoy.org.

To learn more about Bruce Schnack Photography or the "For the Love of Children" ministry, visit www.brucephoto.com. Please note that For the Love of Children clients and referrals are only accepted through Children's Hospital of Minneapolis.

To contact Fred Harburg, e-mail fredharburg@comcast.net.

Platform: The Gift of Your Foundation

Os Guinness, *The Call: Finding and Fulfilling the Central Purpose of Your Life*, Word Publishing (1998).

Power: The Gift of Pressure

To learn more about Jack Groppel's work with the Human Performance Institute, visit www.energyforperformance.com.

Pace: The Gift of Grace to Run Your Race

To discover more about Geoff Miller and Winning Mind, LLC, visit www.thewinningmind.com.

Place: The Gift of Your Environment

To learn more about Medair and the areas it serves, visit www.medair.org.

To find out more about the Center for Fathering, visit www.urbanventures.org/fathering.html.

Prosperity: The Gift of Relationships as Your Legacy

To discover more about Village Schools of the Bible, visit www.vsb.net.

To learn more about the United States African Development Foundation, visit www.adf.gov.

To find out more about the Sleep Out, visit www.bobssleepout.com or www.thesleepout.com.

NOTES

Introduction

1. Larry Julian, *God Is My CEO: Following God's Principles in a Bottom-Line World* (Avon, MA: Adams Media Corporation, 2000), xviii–xix.

Chapter 1. Purpose

1. "U.S. Job Satisfaction Keeps Falling," *The Conference Board* Press Release (February 28, 2005). Extracted from www.conference-board.org/utilities/pressDetail.cfm?press_ID=2582 on March 14, 2007.

2. Ivey Harrington Beckman, "A Significant Touch: How One Halftimer Connected with Her Passion and Touched the World," *The Halftime Report* (December 2002). Extracted from www.halftimereport.org/dec02back.htm on June 21, 2007.

3. Ibid.

4. Os Guinness, *The Call: Finding and Fulfilling the Central Purpose of Your Life* (Nashville, TN: Word Publishing, 1998), 31.

5. Ivey Harrington Beckman, "A Significant Touch: How One Halftimer Connected with Her Passion and Touched the World."

6. Arthur F. Miller, Jr., with William Hendricks, *The Power of Uniqueness: How to Become Who You Really Are* (Grand Rapids, MI: Zondervan, 1999), 31.

7. Ibid., 47 and 231.

Chapter 2. Potential

1. Henry T. Blackaby and Claude V. King, *Experiencing God: Knowing and Doing the Will of God* (Nashville, TN: Lifeway Press, 1990), 15.

Chapter 3. Perspective

1. Kay Miller, "Azteca Angel," *Star Tribune* (March 17, 2007).

2. Ibid.

3. Robert A. Emmons and Michael E. McCullough, *Highlights from the Research Project on Gratitude and Thankfulness*. Extracted from www.psychology.ucdavis.edu/labs/emmons on January 19, 2007.

4. Elizabeth Heubeck, "Boost Your Health with a Big Dose of Gratitude," *WebMD Health*. Extracted from www.women.webmd.com/guide/gratitude-health-boost on February 17, 2008.

5. Rodd Wagner and James K. Harter, Ph.D., *12: The Elements of Great Managing* (New York: Gallup Press, 2006), and *Gallup Management Journal* November 8, 2006 press release.

6. Ibid.

Chapter 5. Power

1. Sid Kirchheimer, "Workaholism: The 'Respectable' Addiction," *WebMD Health*. Extracted from www.webmd.com/balance/guide/workaholism on June 18, 2007.

2. "Gallup Study Indicates Actively Disengaged Workers Cost U.S. Hundreds of Billions Each Year," *Gallup Management Journal* (March 19, 2001). Extracted from www.gmj.gallup.com/content/print/466/Gallup-Study-Indicates-Actively-Disengaged.aspx on May 15, 2007.

Chapter 7. Place

1. "The 2006 Alexander Hamilton Award in Corporate Governance," *Treasury & Risk* (November 2006).

INDEX

ABOUT THE AUTHOR

Larry S. Julian is a successful consultant and speaker who specializes in biblically based leadership development and strategic planning. As an executive coach, he helps business people transcend challenging situations and succeed in the midst of difficulties. He's the author of both the nationally acclaimed business book *God Is My CEO: Following God's Principles in a Bottom-Line World* and of *God Is My Success: Transforming Adversity into Your Destiny*. Larry's passion is to help businesspeople overcome the dilemmas that keep them from experiencing the success God intended.

As president of The Julian Group, Larry uses his experience consulting with the corporate, government, and community sectors in successful speaking, facilitating, and coaching engagements. Over the past several years, he's facilitated hundreds of strategic-planning retreats, team-building retreats, and leadership-development programs. Larry's unique talent is in bringing diverse constituents together in partnerships with a shared vision and a common purpose.

In addition to many churches and nonprofit organizations, his clients have included 3M, General Mills, Mayo Clinic, PepsiCo, and hundreds of other large and small organizations. Larry is also a popular speaker at conferences and churches on the integration of faith and work. He lives in Minneapolis, Minnesota.

Visit www.larryjulian.com for more information.

CONTACT LARRY JULIAN

One-on-One Coaching

Do you need personal coaching to work through a particular dilemma, decision, or gray area? Larry works with a wide range of clients—from CEOs to small business owners—on issues ranging from integrating work and faith to navigating through career and life transitions.

Monthly Group Mentoring Forums

Do you like the dynamics and wisdom a group can bring to your situation? Larry Julian offers a powerful coaching process that saves you both time and money. Larry's group mentoring forums provide a double benefit—you get the benefit of Larry's coaching *and* the collective wisdom of an informal advisory board of like-minded peers.

Speaking Engagements

Looking for a speaker who can craft a program that uniquely addresses the needs of your audience? Whether your goal is to address a specific business need or allow depth and discussion regarding faith and values, Larry can design a program customized for your needs.

Strategic Planning Retreats

Is your organization headed in the right direction? Do your strategies and actions reflect your mission, values, and purpose? Larry Julian conducts leadership team retreats that help participants cut through the distractions that hinder success, enabling the kind of discussion that connects people to the issues and strategies that really matter.

To contact Larry Julian, e-mail him at larry@larryjulian.com.

For additional information visit www.larryjulian.com.